Ask Me Anything…
Letters From Farang

by Scott Mallon

Dedicated to my sister Jennifer.
Somehow she has always remained patient and given me good advice…even though she knows it goes through one ear and out the other.

Also, dedicated to all the inexperienced, clueless Chowderheads around the world that ask for my advice, hear it, and like me, rarely listen.

Introduction

"You can lead a horse to water, but you can't make him drink."

Before I started uploading videos to YouTube in January 2013, I was oblivious to the enormity of the site and how connected it was to the world. Of course I had heard of YouTube, but I rarely watched anything for more than a minute or two and I was still watching network television and cable. Once I realized how prevalent YouTube had become and how quickly the internet was revolutionizing the entertainment industry, I canceled our cable service, and YouTube and Netflix became my primary sources of entertainment.

When my gig with a local boxing promoter ended, the idea of putting up my own videos popped into my head. My original idea was simple; upload videos helping westerners understand Thailand's culture and what it was like living here. People around the world were always looking to move to Thailand, so I figured there might be some interest, but I never dreamed I would go on to rack up millions of views.

It took a few months, but eventually I found my voice and began answering questions. Nothing could prepare me for the sheer volume of questions and comments. Nor was I prepared for the notoriety the channel would bring and how it would affect my personal life. The vast majority of the questions had to do with the relationship problems foreign men had with Thai women. The biggest shock was that many of the men were falling madly in love with prostitutes. Common sense dictates that you don't go looking for love in a whorehouse. If only common sense were more common.

After four years of answering relationship questions and giving the best advice I know how to give, I have concluded that no matter what I say, no matter how much I swear, yell and scream or name call, people will only listen if they want to do so. Even if they are asking for an answer they probably don't really want to hear it.

Table of Contents

Adam -- Absolutely Clueless

Adam

Dear Scott,
Some of the people watching your YouTube videos do not understand Thai culture. Thai girls are generally inhibited sexually, and most non-bargirls do not see sex as an enjoyable activity, they see it as an evil, naughty, nasty chore. When they actually have a real orgasm, they feel ashamed of themselves for enjoying something that is immoral. This is simply a part of the culture, and it is something we need to accept as *farang*.

Regards,
Adam

***

Scott

Adam,
Are you joking? How long have you been in Thailand and what is your experience with Thai women? I've had my share of women here and have been married for a long time and I can assure you, without a doubt, it is definitely not considered a chore by most Thai women. Obviously with some whores, they just want to get it over with and get paid, but about the only thing I've heard is that sex is a tiring activity and the woman needed to be up for it physically.

Say what you will, some Thai women definitely do

1

not feel it is evil and just like most females; they look forward to having orgasms. I can only assume you're a troll or a foreigner who has either never had a good sexual experience with a Thai woman or simply don't know what the hell you're talking about.

It can take time to get Thai women to open up and feel 100% comfortable. Thai women, and many other nationalities of women, are like flowers that need to blossom. Like most people, once they feel secure, they open up and are anything but inhibited. Part of the culture? Dude you are kidding yourself or you've been fed a line of bullshit.

Scott

***

Adam

Hi Scott,

I have been in Pattaya for about two months now. I met my girlfriend at a restaurant in Bangkok the second night I came here, coincidentally, I did not intend to become involved in a long term relationship at all during my stay. I am not even really certain how or why this happened. To be honest, it all just kind of fell together.

It didn't fall together, he took the bait.

We went on an instadate from the restaurant to Hillary Bar 2 and she has not left my side since then. I am actually grateful that she has put up with all my bullshit and has stuck with me despite numerous struggles due to cultural differences.

He was seduced and taken to a bar full of whores. What's next, his girl is different?

Perhaps the wording of my statement was a bit

presumptuous and trollish due to frustration, but I can say (without posting too much personal business) that the culture here seems much more sexually inhibited than back in America, to the point that it can be very highly irritating at times. That being said, I am learning and adapting every day.

Thanks,
Adam

***

Scott

You have been with one Thai woman for two months and already you're making statements about how Thai women aren't into sex? Please...you are clueless and a Chowderhead and I'm being far too kind. I can tell you that without a smidgeon of a doubt you are so far off you might as well be on another planet. While Thai women may be conservative publicly, if you get to know them and they open up emotionally, they are uninhibited.

You are a major league Chowderhead. You hooked up with a Thai chick on your second night in Bangkok, without knowing the language or anything about the culture. To make matters worse, you are calling her your girlfriend. This isn't very bright, but then you say you're grateful she has put up with your bullshit.

What about her being grateful for you?

He should have slept with her, had his fun, and in the morning told her he would be in touch. Instead he went all in.

Also, a decent Thai chick would not be caught dead in the Hillary Bar or Nana Plaza. Taking for granted that she might just have simply decided to go with you to check it

3

out for herself and to be with you, you still have a lot to learn pal and you better watch yourself. Believe me.

Is she a whore, have you given her any money, and is she from Isaan?

Scott

***

Adam

Hey Scott,

She is not a whore, and I have not given her any substantial amount of money, but she is from Isaan. She was at that particular restaurant down the street from Nana because her apartment was less than a block away. In addition, she has friends in the area who work at Hillary.

Rubbish, rubbish, rubbish...take of the blinders!

Now, I may be wrong, but a scammer usually bails after the money gets low, which it certainly has on a few occasions.

Regards,
Adam

***

Scott

"How much is "not substantial?"

***

Adam

Well, not really any directly, except for a few thousand baht here and there for shopping. We also live together, and I did take her to Koh Pha Ngan for the Full Moon Party, if that counts. I was very, very skeptical of her for a while, but now I think she may actually be a keeper.

She speaks very good English and Swedish, and she is much more intelligent than most Isaan girls I have seen thus far, so we don't have any trouble with basic communication. I teach her English every day, which she uses enthusiastically. When she doesn't understand something, she asks, and I explain. She is teaching me Thai, and it seems like she genuinely wants me to learn the language and the culture.

I'm not the kind of guy who puts any woman on a pedestal, and I'm not saying she's my heavenly angel sent by God and that I am so deeply attached that my life depends on our relationship (like some of the idiots you post videos about), but I am saying that I think (and hope) that I've found someone truly worth my time, energy, and commitment.

Men in these situations either think their girl is different or they are different. In this case, neither is true.

Regards,
Adam

***

Scott

Hi Adam,

Does she have a job? If you tell me no, then her stock drops. Here's the thing...if this relationship succeeds it will be one of the very few in this sort of situation. Personally, I think you're out of your mind to get involved with a chick so fast and even more of a Chowderhead for living together. It's easy to find a Thai girlfriend; it's much, much more difficult to get rid of them.

Scott

***

Adam

Dear Scott,

Well… presumably she worked at a small vendor shop for food money and had just recently gotten out of a nine year long-term relationship with another *farang*. She may have paid her rent in other ways out of necessity, but I place no judgment on survival.

Adam

***

Scott

Honestly, I think you are pretty gullible my friend, but at the end of the day all that matters is what makes you happy. While I think it's very important to get to know Thai culture, it is equally important to retain your own.

My guess is you met an Issan woman who is a freelancer and who is basically biding her time with you, but I could be wrong. If she's a decent chick, she'll be willing to work to provide additional income for you as a couple or family. There are many, many married Thai women in the workforce and times have changed.

What did she do with all of her time when she had yet to meet you? How did she live?

If your girl is uneducated or unskilled, then she's probably looking for a savior (not to say she isn't willing to work hard or get a better education) and a way to climb the social ladder. I have to ask though, why would you want a woman incapable of taking care of herself?

What happens if you have children together and you die an untimely death? Then what?

You know close to nothing about the culture (or her), believe me, getting serious with a woman who lives in the lower Sukhumvit area is foolish.

You're in a new relationship. Who knows what will happen, but I wouldn't count on the relationship lasting...give it time and you'll find out. Just make sure not to give too much money or too much of yourself. Nothing at all wrong with testing the waters with her, but why on earth did you ask her to move in with you?

Good luck,
Scott

***

Adam

Hey Scott,

Despite not having a degree, she is quite skilled at cooking. I keep telling her to try and find a job at a restaurant—her food is delicious, even compared with restaurant dishes—but she says the wages are too low even for a chef. I am a freelance writer. Her having an 8-10,000 baht a month salary working 70-80 hours per week with two days off per month, just doesn't make sense. I can potentially make that much or more in a day or two working 4-6 hours per day.

I want to help her find something with reasonable hours and decent pay. Good jobs for Thai girlfriends might be a decent video topic if you haven't covered it already.

Adam

***

Scott

You are starting out behind the eight-ball and trying to change a system here that doesn't want to be changed. To be blunt, as always, why on earth would you get into a serious relationship with an uneducated, jobless chick from a different culture and then move in with her, especially after knowing her such a short time? This makes absolutely no sense to me.

Presumably from what you said, she was involved with a Swede. I'm going to assume she is close to 30 or older. If she has no education, or very little education, and she can't show a work history, unless she gets lucky or is cleaver and ambitious, she will have a hard time finding a decent paying job. There are simply too many educated women who are willing to work for peanuts while they search for a better job or move up in the ranks.

Now...as far as making a video on good jobs for Thai girlfriends, that's not going to happen and I'll tell you why. If a guy hooks up with a chick that is basically unskilled and can't make more than 8-10K baht a month, he's adopting a chick as his girlfriend. Maybe she's a hard worker who is poor. Regardless, you become the guardian angel she relies on and counts on whenever she needs something she is incapable of getting herself. Unless perhaps you start a business here and control it or she's a real go-getter who is driven enough to do more. That adds quite a bit of pressure though, especially once the relationship reaches the point when you are facing marriage or life with a chick that basically lives for you.

I could make a video about your situation, but I can guarantee you many other guys with a fair amount of experience would tell you that you're moving way too fast and are off your rocker for getting involved so soon. It's your life though and I know from experience that no matter how strong an argument I or anyone else makes, you need to figure it out for yourself.

You're falling into the trap so many guys fall into; you think that because this is Thailand everything is different. It's not. Assuming you had your shit together and were from the US or Europe, you would want a woman with potential and who is capable of not only taking care of herself but also of you if necessary But you come here and perhaps because you believe that the majority of Thais are dirt poor, you change your guidelines.

She has you believing you need to take care of her because this is the Thai way. What about your way? You barely know her and you're in a ready-made relationship. Next she's going to tell you that you need to get married and pay 500K baht sin sod.

I can understand falling for a woman who has very little going for herself in life. Once you find this out, then what? Find her a job, help her balance her budget and make sure she stays on track? It's hard enough carrying on a relationship with a woman who has her own act together.

Add in that she is from a completely different culture, a culture you know very little about, and like I said, you're starting out behind the eight-ball.

Scott

***

Adam

Well said Scott;

It is kind of funny how that happened. I took her home the first night. It was fun, so I took her to Pha Ngan, and after that, we just kind of stuck together. We had the discussion one day regarding being in a relationship, and she said that she had some feelings, and would love to be my girlfriend. I kind of agreed, because to be honest, I had never been with a woman 1/10th as good looking as her back in America. In addition, at that time, she was incredibly nice and accommodating and she helped me out constantly in every way she could. And she still does, to a large extent. The only exception is the whole job thing.

Now, I'm not going to paint a rosy picture of the situation once we started actually living in an apartment together. It has been a rather interesting roller coaster ride of emotions, for both of us. It has been at the breaking point several times, but it has generally gotten better as time has progressed. I hate to admit it, but now I feel a certain pity for her. She seems so vulnerable, and as hard as I might try to fight it, my male protector instinct kicks in quite hard for this one.

And even if I did break up with her now, I would have to set her (or myself) up with another apartment before I did because I wouldn't feel right otherwise. She might just have some nasty friends in the mafia or in the police who would come to collect if I just left her in the dirt.

For the moment, it is going well, though, except for some minor personal issues I'd rather not discuss in a public. So I'm winging it, currently. I'm planning on traveling elsewhere soon. That may be the true test of our relationship. That is, whether or not she is willing to accompany me to a different country, and actually explore the world.

Adam

***

Scott

She will probably go wherever you want to go, at least temporarily because you're her meal ticket. You are putting her on a pedestal despite what you say. She might be good looking, great. Bang her and split and maybe see her once in a while, but there is no reason to get seriously involved with her right away and let her move in.

Your relationship is a rollercoaster - it shouldn't be. It should be as mellow as you want it to be. You pity her when the truth is you most definitely should not. You're what's known as Captain Save a Ho and this applies whether she's a straight up whore or not. She's a leech and you're not necessarily THE GUY as much as you are HER TURN.

She might have some nasty friends or in the mafia? You have been watching too many movies. For the most part, a girl like this is someone that no one in the mafia is going to go out of their way for. Not only this, where are all her friends when she needs money and a place to stay? If they were so close to her that they would harm you they would make sure she's well fed and has a place to stay. It's your life but considering everything you don't know and what is known, I would proceed with caution.

Buck up buttercup, the fun (if you can call it that) has just begun. If she gives you a smidgeon of trouble, be kind, give her 10,000 baht and tell her it is over. You'll thank me later.

She was fine before she met ya and she'll be fine when you're gone.

Scott

Final Thoughts

In my opinion, Adam is in no way ready for relationship with their woman. He would have been better off seeing this girl once in a while, have a little fun, while at the same time biding his time, waiting for her to show her hand. What I think about his situation is irrelevant though. He's already knee deep in it.

Trust takes time. Falling in lust can happen in a second, a minute, or an hour, but it takes time to see how a person acts and reacts to situations. It takes time to figure out their personality, their quirks, likes, dislikes and their motivations. Only time will demonstrate whether she is trustworthy or will turn on him at the first sign of distress.

A man comes to Bangkok, and heads to the heart of the whoring zone. On his second night, he meets a woman who immediately becomes his girlfriend. She hasn't left his side since they met, and apparently, this is love. She has no job and expects him to take care of her since 'This is the Thai way.' She's been in a prior relationship with a foreigner and has no means of supporting herself with a livable wage. She sounds like a real catch.

I have but one suggestion—AIM HIGHER.

Andreas - I Can't See Clearly Now...

Andreas

Hello Scott!

I found your videos on YouTube and want to thank you for doing all this work and giving out this information about Bangkok, Thailand. Well, your videos are also a little therapy for me. *(Wonderful, now in addition to being someone who makes crappy little videos for YouTube, I am a therapist who isn't paid $150 an hour.)*

They give me an interesting insight into the Thai society that I did not know until now; even I though am involved with Thailand since 1993.

I am from Austria and run a little business here. Actually, this is going since 1993 and this was the second time I came to Thailand. The first time was some years earlier on a Southeast Asia trip for business matters.

Anyway, since then I was in and out of Bangkok every year at least once. I learn to love the Thai people. I mostly know well-to-do Thai people who run big businesses in Bangkok. I know no one from Isaan. I love the food and the religion too. Besides my many other businesses and private activities I am practicing Vipassana meditation on a regular basis.

Well, by now you might see that I am not the usual customer of your site (so to say). I am not at all involved with the bar / prostitution scene. For years, I have different girlfriends on and off, normal girls who have their own job and place. I never really lived with a woman in Austria or in Thailand, even when I had relationships last three or more years at a time.

Two years ago, I met a Thai lady over here in Austria at my friends' house (actually she was Austrian born in Thailand and living 25 years over here). I joined up with her. She also was a Buddhist and I liked the way she presented herself to me. She was very humble and also a vegetarian.

(Wow, Buddhist, humble, and a vegetarian! She sounds like a keeper!)

I had an extremely harmonious time with her. Usually in all my other relationships, sooner or later some quarrels would arise and then the relationships would drift apart. Well, as I met her I promised to myself to give my best with her. She would never question my decisions, even many times giving me the power to decide what we would do or where we would go.

This last sentence is extremely elucidating, giving us insight how he interacts with women. What has become of men today? While I am all for discussion, I am a firm believer Thai women want men to take the reins and make decisions.

She was 46 when I met her. Her first ten years she was married to a guy she claimed was not a very good person. She had no feelings for him and told me she was with him only for the visa (10 years).

Why is it so many Thai women claim they were with a man who was not a very good person? She spent ten years with a guy who was not a very nice person and she had no feelings for him. Although many Thai women have a hard time admitting guilt or fault, sorry, I don't buy it. This is one of many warning signs Andreas did not heed.

After her divorce, she moved in with a rich businessman. She lived in his house and he took care for all the expenses. He gave her pocket money and she would freely take extra cash as

she liked. She told me that once they did a three weeks holiday in Thailand and spend 10,000 Euros) and her own money (1100 Euros she works in a kitchen full time job).

This woman is very clearly a moocher. She earns very little but wants and expects a grand lifestyle in exchange for her time and the triangle between her legs. If more men went and hard a tug instead of caving into women like this, there would be far less men whining about getting taken by women.

She would send money back to Thailand, to Isaan. Her money was spent by all the members of her very large patchwork family on *sanuk* (fun) and not on building a house as she intended. Her mother built a shack as said the rest was gone.

This businessman put her as a manager in his company. The company had a bankruptcy some years later and she had to face the court. I was told the court found him faulty, not her, so she was off the hook.

Andreas noted he is unlike many of those who write me and he is correct. He is even more oblivious! The warning signs are all there yet he still seems to believe this woman. Of course, his situation with her is different. If a woman is talking smack about a man she

has lived with for ten years, she'll talk smack about you and it shows her lack of class.

First, she had me believe she could pay a 500,000 Euro debt she had. Later, I found out it was only some court fees, but this also she did not want to do for her man. She always claimed she loves him but she walked out of him.

All her girlfriends over here would live with way older guys. They were not very wealthy blokes, but they paid everything. Most of them are alcoholics. The girls treat them like shit, not like a husband, and do this with a smile in their faces. Some of these women have a gik (boyfriend) besides their husbands. Well, a lot of warning signs if you look close, as I should have I sensed what she had in stock for me the time to come.

The warning signs are shining brightly but when a man is in the midst of romance, there is usually a thick fog of lust surrounding him.

After one year, she was living in a bad part of town. I brought her over to my area where I have an extra apartment and offered it for her to rent it from me, but for a love price only 200 Euro a month. This place is a three-bedroom, new renovated, free hold apartment.

She agreed to pay my rent and the housing fees. I would not live there but visited her often and slept there regularly. Mostly, she came overnight to my place. She also would eat at my place and in her workplace.

Well, as I said, I had a very harmonious time. I always told her that marriage would be not for me. She likes the free lifestyle much more, with her own place, etc., not like all her

other girlfriends.

17

She wants her cake and to eat it too. For her, a relationship with Matthias is as convenient as a relationship can be. She has complete freedom to do what she wants and if she wants, she can be with other men. She has a dirt cheap, nice place to live in exchange for what banging Andreas whenever she feels like it. She has her freedom, and if she wants, she sees other men. From her history, I would think she is also obtaining money from them. To me, this woman is as close to a whore as a woman can be.

Once she was here, I getting more and more emotional with her without noticing it. I was completely open to her and really thought we would stay like this forever. We were family, although not married. She always said that she has no financial problems and was very happy the way the things were arranged.

At the beginning of last November I came to her place and with a smile she told me that she was finishing with me and going to another guy because this guy promised her to marry her.

Imagine my shock. I was out of order. After I tried to convince her and showed her that I really loved her very much, she agreed to rethink her decision. About two weeks later, she told me that now she pushed me out of her system and she would never come back to me. Also, she would leave the apartment to move over to this guy's house. This man is 55 (I am 49 and a fitness freak, well trained, highly active. For most of the days, she would receive three orgasms a day, honestly, no joke.)

He had a heart surgery, his body looks shit, and he is a dirty fellow with not much of an education. He is a drinker, has two divorces, and a blood sickness that requires him to take drugs that have as side effect, impotence.

Andreas just does not get it. She's not into him. Even if she was, this particular woman still might stray for the cash and prizes. Also, he thinks he is a good catch and while he might be, women have their own way of thinking. Seems to me this woman is out for the orgasms and the Do-Re-Mi. BTW – making a woman orgasm might be the key to her heart, then again, she might just need the relief. Also, while Andreas might be exceptionally skilled between the sheets and get her off like a rocket, she might just be a good actress or easy to satisfy. For all he knows, the orgasms and cheap apartment might be the only reason she keeps him around!

The only thing this man has is a house and he offered it to her to stay there for free. But it is in a faraway place, now she needs to travel to her job, more than an hour each way (from here it was only 20 min). We had a last conversation and I really wanted to know why she left me. There was no arguments at all, believe me.

Over and over again I told her I loved her very much. Suddenly she was very angry and told me, 'You always ring me up in the evening asking me to visit you at your place but you never give me any money. I do not need a guy like this.' A woman always needs some extra cash but you never give it to me. If you handed me 1500 Euro every month, I would stay with you and drop that other guy. I only want a normal marriage (like all her friends) but you don't want this.'

We agreed on this so I was in the biggest shock of my life. I lost three kilos straight and needed six weeks to get back to almost normal.

I met another couple. The wife is also from Thailand and worked in the same kitchen and my ex called her sister. She asked her why she left me and she said it was because I did not give her money. It's so hardcore. She lived with me for two years only to finally get money or all her expenses paid by me. It is so unbelievable. All the people who knew her including my family could not believe it. In this story I had no financial loss at all but the pain on my soul

was much bigger.

As I told you, I am into meditation and this helped me to recover pretty soon. This was the craziest thing that ever happened to me. Now I laugh about it and if I ever meet another Thai lady again, I will be very careful to open myself too much as we never know when she switches off the light. Sure, I never will give them any money and all this is far away from Thailand or the Pattaya bar scene.

If you feel good and have time I would be happy to get your view on this.

Thank you.

***

Scott

Is it really so surprising? This woman admitted to you she was only with a guy for the visa and with a guy basically for the cash. Did you think she was an angel? In Thai culture, or any other culture for that matter, her lifestyle was completely unacceptable to a decent Thai / person. I would have run, seriously. Either that or simply screwed her occasionally and kept my distance.

Be lucky she did not sting you for your life savings.

Scott

***

Andreas

Hello Again Scott !

Thank you for your answer mate. Your videos you are absolutely right. I really thought she was an angel. A part of me is just like that, the old idealist, even as I work business with people who often are not really so nice.

Love is blind and has rendered many a good man senseless.

Hey, she meditated with me and had an almost three meter wide Buddha shrine. I told the whole story to our Theravada monk (very serious forest tradition); he smiled and told me, 'Hey she does not meditate as instructed, she only dreams with her mind.'

This man knows what he's talking about (but all that knowledge came to me after she left).

Also, this Thai monk has a sound knowledge about the local Thai women—even he by nature is not married. Once I spoke with him several times, I was surprised how strong and clear his judgment was and how true it proved in the end.

Maybe I should become a monk. By nature he is not married? No, he is a monk! He is committed (supposedly) to a life of celibacy!

Her lifestyle was completely unacceptable to a decent Thai / person.

All her girlfriends hang out with guys, in my opinion,

mostly for the security money.

I don't blame them as they are poor at home but once my story was known in the local community, and I made sure by telling the whole thing to some ladies, they spread the truth. Many were really disgusted. I could see it in their faces as they know the way I treated her, with heart, not with cash, rather to try to create opportunities for her (that she did not want).

After all this I made sure she lost her face a 100% within her own group or simply screwed her once in a while and kept my distance. In the begin, I really thought to keep it that way but she made sure to be always around me and I am also not that kind of person so slowly I was drowned into it without noticing it.

Her circle of friends was probably laughing. What Andreas fails to realize is some Thai women (or any nationality) will lie through their teeth with a straight face and absolutely no concern for a man's feelings. They can turn it on and turn it off, playing the part whenever need be. In their limited little pea brains, the end justifies the means. Money is number one and is their key to survival and climbing up the social ladder. Friends, even mothers and grandmothers will flat out lie to male visitors who possibly can provide a financial windfall, and I have yet to see one riddled with guilt because of it.

"Oh no, my daughter wants a husband very much, she no have boyfriend."

In the meantime, the man you think is her brother is actually her husband. Once you pay out a chunk of money to the family, the woman no longer needs or wants you around—unless they think they can continue milking the cow dry. Men need to wake up. If it seems to be too good to be true, it probably is.

I am very, very lucky, I think, but as I would not marry anyway. It's just too much of a burden to a usually happy lifestyle and we are not sure how things would work out one or two years from now. Maybe she thought I will try my best with him for one year and when I offered her the apartment she thought to be near to the goal. In fact, she did not really understand much about how I function with cash or business. Well, she understood her way into my emotions. Anyway, I would not give any cash to her whatsoever but I helped her with many economical things, just not involving my own funds only, only my knowledge.

I think in the very end she must be completely pissed off and stressed out because she did not reach her final goal, marriage (means I pay her shit) or cash in hand forever. In my deep heart, I never believe I can buy love. If a women stays with me, the financial has to be a mutual agreement (like we pay half-half), but not a one way situation. If I would go to Thailand for a girl, sure, I should help her until she is here and can work and make her own money. All this would be too much stress though and I will never ever even consider it.

Life is a learning process. Many guys already know what I had to learn in this situation. By telling my story I learned that many guys here have divorced and bled for years or for the rest of their lives, emotionally and financially, mostly with local or Eastern European women. I am now a little more compassionate if I hear such stories. In these regards, men are far weaker than women.

So again, thanks Scott for your time and your direct

style of saying things. Keep it up that way. Somebody must be really off their head falling in love with a Thai hooker. Maybe it was you that said in your video or in somebody else's that the real hardcore sex tourist would never fall for hookers. They have their good time, they enjoy themselves, and pay and the story is the same as in all brothels and bars all over the world.

There are many guys who come to Thailand who are not as profound in their decisions and as the Thai ladies give them the perfect girlfriend experience, they fall and pay, pay, and pay.

All the best,
Andreas

Final Thoughts
The sender seems like a nice guy, perhaps too nice and my guess is he's been taken advantage more than once. In many instances, especially in dealing with whores, nice guys are flushed down the toilet, leaving them floating in an abyss, questioning why love is so cruel. I almost feel sorry for him. Almost because he is a man and thus he is responsible for his own actions. The writing was on the wall and it couldn't have been written more clearly. Yet, he was blinded by passion. Had he acted like a man, taking charge, telling her how things were going to be, and refusing any nonsense, she would have fallen in line or moved on to some other sucker. He allowed her to control his emotions and his life. Although he suffered little financially, he paid in time and with his emotions, two precious commodities that are limited in supply.

Find a woman who has her own money and can

support herself. At least you know there is a good chance your money is not her first priority.

This is a perfect example of a woman being out for herself and caring little for her partner. She is a user to the nth degree, a woman who makes men pay the price for being too kind and having too much desire.

Brad - Can You Set Me Up With the Girl in Your Video?

Brad

Dear Scott,

First, I have a lot of experience in Thailand and lived there for 15 years in Bangkok and Chiangmai. I would like to know if the pretty girl wearing braces and a t-shirt (hair tinted reddish) in the *Pork Street Stall* video is living someplace where you could find her again. I would send you $100.00 if you could get me her email and cell phone number providing she is single. I speak Thai pretty well and would like to contact her. I would trust you and pay you before you get the contact details.

Thanks,
Brad

***

Scott

I know exactly where to find her, but she is married and works with her husband. Even if she was single though, I wouldn't do this. I'm not a matchmaker, I know her quite a bit better than I know you, and since I don't know you from a hole in the wall, I wouldn't even consider it.

***

Brad

I understand and thanks. The fact that she is married rules out my interest and I wasn't suggesting you were a matchmaker. Duh! I would assume you know her much better than I do!

Duh? WTF? This guy is already rubbing me the wrong way.

Like I may have said, I lived there for 15 years, I am fluent in the language and culture and I am a practicing Tibetan (not the Thai) Buddhism.

Whatever gave this guy the notion that I might somehow be interested in knowing he's a Tibetan Buddhist? Did he think this would mean something to me? Good for him, he's a Tibetan Buddhist. And? So what?

A nice thing you can learn from the Thai Buddhism—although it conjuncts with a kind of unnecessary phoniness—is being more non-confrontational. Tibetans call our speech the speech door, and it is a veritable weapon, like a knife. It might behoove you to be aware of this.

It might behoove him to fuck off because at this point, I think he's a douche bag.

It begins with assuming less about people you don't know. You can evolve into being careful, even more compassionate in your approach to people.

Buddhism says patience is the greatest of all austerities. Furthermore, we generate karma through three doors. The first is the body (our actions), our speech (what we say) and our minds (what we think). So be careful what you rush to think about, or do, or say to someone as you may unwittingly generate karma that is not in your best interest. This happens if it is not based on compassion, free of bias and by your best interest. I mean your happiness in this and in your future lives. This is not to assume you believe in the notion of reincarnation. Reality remains reality…regardless.

All the Best,
Brad

P.S. I should add (for balance) that I have watched several of your videos and think you offer a good service, especially speaking of good Thai women, which it seems so many of the world's males appear to believe don't exist. It's very sad what goes on in Thailand (sex trade).

***

Scott

Dear Bradley,
What do you call it when one person asks another to get the email address and cell phone number of a random women they don't know? You can phrase it however you want, but I am not a matchmaker nor do I wish to be one. It's certainly not a big deal to me but quite frankly, I don't want to waste my time doing this sort of thing nor do I wish to set some young girl up with a guy I don't know. You might be surprised at how often men ask me to do this sort of thing and I always decline. You want a woman, go out and get her yourself.

As far as everything else, I am confrontational when I feel it appropriate. Your beliefs are your beliefs; don't try to impose them on me.

The other day a guy told me I should make higher class videos instead of the most recent one I made. I'll tell you what I told him; while I understand you may have good intentions, if I want your advice, I'll ask for it.

Final Thoughts

One of my many rules is to refrain from getting involved in matters of the heart. This may come off as a contradiction considering I answer men's questions about relationships, however, my answering their questions is no different from them going to a buddy and asking him what he thinks. Once I am asked to start sticking my beak in as a matchmaker, pimp, vetting agent or any other job title that parallels these, I draw the line.

Men (and Thai women) have asked me to hook them up, act as a translator, and in one case, a guy on an expat forum asked me to call his love interest to make sure she didn't get back with her boyfriend that had supposedly beat her prior to their break-up. Of course, when I politely declined, the guy called me every name in the book. He had yet to meet her in person and had been speaking to her for a month.

A week later he wrote back apologizing and I told him to fuck off and take responsibility for his own life. There are several things in life that bother me and failing to take responsibility for one's actions are one of them. You got a problem with your woman, handle your business and leave me out of it. Getting involved in these sorts of affairs is a waste of my time and energy.

Que sera, sera, whatever will be will be. If the relationship was meant to be, it will be.

If Brad was a buddy of mine and I knew him to be a decent human being and a gentleman, I would have thrown him the assist. Brad had never communicated with me though. So he saw a video on YouTube, decided he wanted to meet the girl in it, and out of the blue, from halfway across the world wrote me to arrange the hook-up. Okay, fine. His politely asking for assistance would have been forgiven, but instead of shutting his pie hole he felt the need to give his religious advice, crossing a sacred line.

He contacted me, I responded and he didn't appreciate my response. Too bad, cupcake!

Bruce - Never a Thanks or Thank You!

Bruce

Hey Scott,

I would like to share my story with you about my experiences in Thailand and my Thai wife. My name is Bruce. I am 45 and live in Australia with my wife Nong. She is 35 years old and from Sukhothai.

Back in 2010 a friend and I took a holiday in Phuket. We did the usual tourist things and hit the bars to meet up with the Thai ladies. One day I decided to try out a Thai massage. This is where I met Nong. To my surprise, there was no happy ending. I had heard so many stories, but in this case, there was no happy ending.

The next day I went back to the same girl (great massage). She didn't offer anything else, so I thought she was different.

First mistake, assuming she was different!

I thought she was a good Thai girl. So I thought I would try to ask her out (her English was very good). First, she said no, but I persisted and finally she said yes. I met her after work at 11pm and we grabbed a bite to eat. Some of her friends came along, but after the meal, she wanted to go down to the beach to meet some more of her friends. We drank and talked on the beach until 2:30 AM and had a great time. When it was time to go home, she was planning on going back to her place (alone), but it was such a long walk, I told her to stay with me.

Such a gentleman!

She said no, and then eventually said yes. That night she slept with her clothes on and we talked until early in the morning. This went on for four nights until we eventually made love. I think it had been a while for her.

It was then I noticed her back was covered in tattoos. I actually thought they were pretty cool. After three days, I had to return to Australia, but I promised her I would return to see her again. Four months passed and I was talking to her every second day on the phone. Then she started asking me for money. First, I said no, and then she told me 'Many men want to take care of me.' This is a phrase I have never forgotten.

She works at a massage parlor, is covered in tattoos, and she is asking for money after three days of being together. Red lights should be flashing in his head and once she started asking for cash, the relationship type should have changed. He should have never assumed she was different in the first place, but once she asked for money and then told him she had many men wanting to take care of her, it should have been a no-brainer.

I started sending her $500 per month. Some months I would send a little less.

Second mistake and this one makes him a Grade-A Chowderhead!

I returned back to Phuket after four months. She was still working. We stayed in Phuket for two nights then caught the bus to Sukhothai to stay at her home and meet her family. It was good fun and I stayed there for four weeks. We decided to go shopping and then she started.

"Can you buy this, can you buy that?" she asked.

The only thing I bought for her was a notebook so we could talk on Skype and email each other. While we were in Thailand together we applied for a three month tourist visa for her to go to Australia. I returned home and a week later, her visa was granted. I picked her up from the airport and took her back home. While she was in Australia, I took her everywhere. I was working at the time, so we went out mainly on weekends and after work. I noticed her checking out other men, smiling and staring at them. Some of them were older than me. This was in shopping centers, clubs, just about everywhere we went together. It was to the extent they would come up to her wanting to buy her a beer or to start a conversation while I was standing next to her. I was so pissed off I asked her what she was doing.

"I have eyes. I can look, I have a mouth, and I can talk. I love you only," she said.

After three days, he brings her to Australia, shows her around and then in an effort to show her gratitude, she flirts with other men. A polite, classy woman in love would have never done this or at the very least made a supreme effort to ignore the advances or flat out tell the men Bruce was her boyfriend.

This went on for so long and then arguments started.

It went on because he allowed it to go on. Make no mistake about this.

We went to a Muay Thai show and she was not even watching the fights, she just checked out other men in the crowd. I couldn't say anything because it would only end in an argument and tears and ruin a good night. I just kept remembering what she said, "I love you and only you," which I think was bullshit. I can also tell anybody I love them and not mean it. Three months went by and she returned home.

Okay, a woman is going to do what a woman wants to do, sometimes whether her man likes it or not. If she gave a guy a quick look because he was handsome, this might be forgivable. However, checking men out, staring at them, smiling at them, and then talking to them, is tasteless and in my books, grounds for sending her ass back to Thailand.

She would have whined and cried, and perhaps she could have been forgiven ONCE, but to tell him she has eyes and can look, and a mouth and can talk is too much to tolerate. Crying or not, her ass should have been on the next plane. It takes a man with a pair of balls to stand up to a manipulative woman like this, but her flirtatious nature was s a huge warning sign. Shipping her home would have alleviated his future headaches. And yet, the pussy and the tears were too much for him to overcome.

Since then I have taken five trips to Thailand and she has taken two to Australia; once on a three month visa and once on a six month visa. Between her coming to see me, she lived in her home taking care of her Mum. I continued sending her $500 per month. While in Thailand, she told me she had previously been married to a Thai man, but the marriage ended after a few weeks because of money issues and also because he thought she was seeing another man.

Warning, warning, warning! Buyer beware!

While I was in Thailand I bought her a new motorbike, a refrigerator, a freezer, an air-conditioner, a satellite dish and a wall unit for her television, but it was never enough.

Of course not, she is a prostitute and in her mind, if you are going to be with her, you are going to need to pay, pay, and pay. She wants as much milk from the cow as she can get.

When I was in Thailand, I always kept busy helping around the house. I also took her mother, niece, myself and younger sister to Chiang Rai and Chiang Mai (a beautiful place). I paid for everything, right down to the bowls of noodles for her mother at the markets. You know what, no one from her family ever said thanks or thank you, they just grunted or groaned. I didn't think thanking me would have been so difficult, but it was.

I decided to look past all the lies and the lack of appreciation and got married in a traditional Thai wedding in March of 2013. I gave her 360,000 baht (approximately $10,000 USD) but her mother thought it wasn't enough. This was all I was going to give her though.

The night before the marriage we had a karaoke night. A Thai man tried to pick up my mother and up she was very upset. My mother flew to Thailand to be at the marriage, not to hook up with a strange, drunk Thai. He had way too much to drink and when I told my wife to be about it, she told me I didn't understand Thai people. I was so pissed off. I let it go as we were going to be married the next day. My wife-to-be continued drinking and singing like nothing had happened. I was shocked she would talk to us like that the night before we were to be married.

It's one issue after another. Bruce's lack of action, or lack of balls to phrase it more appropriately, is what has him in this dysfunctional relationship. Despite knowing exactly how this woman is, he continues to stay with her.

How much clearer does it need to be that this woman and her family are no-class pieces of shit? Maybe she needs to screw another man in front of him to snap him out of this nightmare. Her attitude is horrible and one he would not experience if her were with a woman of substance.

After we were married, I caught her lying about money many times. Once I asked how much money she had and she told me 20,000 baht. I was positive she had more than this, but she showed me her bank book and the balance was 20,000 baht. I asked if she had another bank book and she said she had no others. I wanted to know happened to all the money from the wedding. She told me she spent it all on the wedding. I still wasn't sure.

One night when she went to a funeral, I found a key to a cupboard. I decided to take a look and sure enough, there was another bank book. The balance was 300,000 baht.

When she got home, I asked her again how much money she had in the bank. Against she replied 20,000 baht. I told her I thought she was lying and again she denied having more money. I gave her the opportunity to tell me the truth, but it wasn't happening. I called her a liar and told her I looked in the cupboard. Her only response was that I shouldn't be looking. That's all she said and she didn't want to talk about it anymore.

Another problem… does this really come as a surprise? When will this guy learn? Apparently, he is never going to acknowledge the problems he has with her. First, she's lying. This is huge. Second, her attitude is piss-poor. Third, he should have cut his losses and left after she asked him for money. Obviously, he's a glutton for punishment.

She has a taxi driver friend in Bangkok and she always uses him to take her to and from the airport. Every time we're in the taxi together, after not seeing her for 4-6 months, they have their own conversation in Thai. One time I thought I would start talking with her about what she had been doing while we had been apart and a minute later, I can see her getting angry and bored.

"Can you please stop talking to me? I am boring with you," she said.

She just continued her conversation with the driver. Four weeks later we were married and I returned home.

I can only assume he enjoys the pain. The second she said she's bored with him, he should have said, 'That's it, goodbye.' After being away from one another for 4 - 6 months you would think she would be happy to see him and would be unable to keep her hands off him. How many times does she need to disrespect him before he stands up for himself and takes action?

In October 2013, I returned back to Thailand. This time I tried to look at things a little bit differently, for as they say, love is blind. I arrived at the airport and waited for her; she was an hour late. Her conversation with the taxi driver starts again and I just sit there not wanting to cause any trouble. That night in the motel, she had 250 ml of coconut sex oil and it was half empty. We were not off to a great start.

She said she bought it at a bus station about four hours north of Bangkok.

"What did you do with it," I asked.

"I drank it," she said.

So she expected me to believe she drank a half a bottle of coconut oil in four or five hours. Back at her home she never drank this oil again. Did she think I'm stupid?

Yes, she thinks he's stupid and a pushover, which he has clearly showed to be true.

Things were about to change the way I feel about her.

And why should I believe this? From his proven track record?

While we were in Thailand together, she was granted a permanent visa to live with me in Australia. I had enough of her lies though. I wanted to tell her this, but not while I was living in her house. So I waited until I returned home from Thailand. It was impossible to talk and argue with her at her home. She would start crying, and then her mum would start yelling in Thai. I could never win arguing with her at her home, just like with the taxi driver. So I waited until I was going home. At the airport, I told her how I had enough of her lying. Of course, she cried and then I flew home.

She is now back working in Phuket.

When I'm in Thailand I feel they treat me on the same level as the pigs she takes care off behind her house. The exact order of importance: mum, brothers, sisters, niece, nephew, friends, ex-husbands, ex-boyfriends, all other Thai people, pigs, and then me, the person who gives here money and takes care of her family.

The more this guy told me, the more I started to believe he was a eunuch. One of the first rules I told my wife was that I must come first. If this didn't happen, our marriage would not work. Everyone else comes last, I come first. This changed once she gave birth to our two sons, but considering they're our children, this is understandable in most cases. If a woman treats a man like one of the pigs and he allows it to continue, she has no respect for him and he has no respect for himself.

When my wife introduces me to other people, she always uses the Thai word *fan (*boyfriend) instead of husband. She said this is normal.

Although the word faen is used in reference to a boyfriend or girlfriend, women also use the word in lieu of saami, or husband, when referring to their partner.

After we were married, we planned on living together in Thailand when I turned fifty as I would then qualify for a retirement visa. I understand I will never fit in or be Thai, but it would be nice to be treated as an equal.

Hope to hear from you soon. Keep up the great work.

Take care,

Bruce

***

Scott

Hey Bruce,

There are many types of women, but I believe they can be narrowed down into two types if you look closely.

There are those who genuinely care enough about their man to be sorry about the wrongs they've committed or hurt they've caused. Then there are those who will say they are sorry just to shut the man up. Occasionally, even the best women will do this. Most do it in order to make things easier for themselves and simply give in, but the difference is there are little things and there are unforgivable actions. Disrespecting your mother is unforgivable. Also, if she's disrespected you and your mother once, she will eventually do this again. This is not typical behavior of a decent Thai woman who was brought up properly. There are women who are brought up poor who would never think about asking their man for money in the beginning of a relationship so wealth has little to do with it.

My wife was brought up in the South and while her family wasn't poor, they certainly weren't rich. Many southern Thais have rubber trees which generates a decent income by Thai standards. In the beginning, I think the only thing she let me pay for was her English school and this was because I was giving her a hard time about how she spoke English. She spoke decent English but I wanted her to improve her grammar to differentiate herself from other Thais who speak pigeon-English. She did so and she and we rarely speak Thai with one another.

If you are like most people, you value marriage and this is what makes things difficult. Unfortunately, just like some westerners, some Thais do not place a high value on marriage and are only concerned with what they can get out of their partner. I am hardly the person to give up on a marriage when there are problems, but there is no point being miserable for the rest of your life when you are still relatively young and have many years ahead of you.

Good luck, Merry Christmas, and let me know if you come to Bangkok.

Scott

***

Bruce

Hi Scott

Thank you so much for your advice, it is very much appreciated and it is good to hear your opinion. It will sound so stupid but I was actually starting to think everything my wife said and did was okay because she would always finish with I love you and only you. Because of this she thought everything would be fine, but now I understand it is not okay to be treated with disrespect.

When I met my wife she wanted to continue doing massage in Phuket. I told her I wanted her to finish working there and I would take care of her. So she moved back home Sukhothai. She told that many years ago she worked in Taiwan at a tissue factory and this is how she saved money to buy her house. Then somehow, she moved to Bangkok to study massage.

She is the first Thai lady I have been with. I had a Chinese girlfriend before, but permanently living in Australia, I have a thing for Asians.

I think Thai people take care of Thai people first. Maybe not in all circumstances, but certainly in my own. I am pretty sure she is not from the Isaan province as her brothers and sisters, all nine of them, live a stone's throw from each other ten kilometers south of Khirimat. Her Mum has always lived with her or her sister next door.

They are a very close family.

I think you are right if I tell her how it is going to be she is only going to tell me what I want to hear and then turn around the next day and do the same thing again, telling me she loves me and only me. This has happened so many times before.

Fool me once, shame on you. Fool me twice, shame on me. This guy allowed this girl to trample all over him as a man and kept coming back for more.

She got her permanent visa in September to live with me in Australia. I told her she cannot come to Australia until we sort things out and I am sure she will not pay for her own airfare to Australia as she likes money very much. But if she really loved me, wouldn't she take the chance and buy a ticket anyway? I know I would!

If a woman is in love, a thousand horses couldn't stop her from being with her man.

She has to come to Australia before March 30 or her visa will be cancelled. I think I would rather be happy and single than married and unhappy. Sorry to put my problems on to you, but it does help to understand a little bit more. I would like to send you a photo sometimes it is easier to put a face to the mail. How can I do this?

Thank you very much,
Bruce

Not the brightest bulb of the lot, is he? I hesitate to call a man stupid, but he is definitely not a rocket scientist. The equation is simple and never changes; man meets money hungry slut, slut does anything she can to get his money, when money is no longer forthcoming, she leaves.

***

Scott

Bruce,

The video about you and her, minus names and other specifics, goes up tomorrow.

Are you still with her, and if so, do you intend to stay with her? Honestly, I would have cut her ass off before you got married. She would have got one shot, and then if she didn't shape up, it would have been goodbye. You can't allow a girl like her any leeway because she'll take advantage of it. In other words, she needs to be kept on a short leash.

Whether a massage parlor girl, bar girl, or a girl working at a bank, sometimes you never really know until you've been with them for a stretch. Even the good ones can end up being rotten, so don't be too hard on yourself or let her get to you. Some Thai women count on foreigners being soft-hearted. Thai men can be brutal with them. Many Thai women blame the men for being bad when the truth is, the men simply didn't want to put up with their shit.

Scott

***

Bruce

Hi Scott,
Here are some photos of me and my wife.

Thanks,
Bruce

Honestly, I was less than impressed with his woman's

looks, especially knowing what I know about her. Here are the facts: she is a money-hungry masseuse who gives happy endings, she will do just about anything for gifts and money and she's disrespectful not only to him, but to his mother. In just about any man's book—at least any man with a sack—this makes her a whore and a disrespectful bitch, two negative attributes in any relationship.

No matter how good looking the woman, no man should put up with the shit she dished out. She is definitely not the marrying type...unless you're this guy.

***

Bruce

Hi Scott

I have watched your videos and you are right, unfortunately I did not view them earlier. When I finally watched your videos, I realized how stupid I was to let it go on for so long. But I could not see it at the time.

Ray Charles could have seen this broad's intentions a mile before he entered her vagina.

Scott, I have finished with her and learned a valuable lesson. I have moved on from her and it is all good.

Thanks for everything
Bruce

***

Bruce,

Hi Scott

I told her right from the start of the relationship I would finish with her if she ever went back to massage

44

and this is what she has done. She can disrespect me as much as she wants, maybe I will forgive her, but to disrespect my 70-year-old Mum who flew to Thailand to be at our wedding… she hasn't got a snowballs chance in hell of being forgiven. I have lost all trust in her with all her lies and disrespect.

Again, knowing his track record, I do not believe this.

I am pretty sure we are legally married in Australia, because we registered the marriage in Thailand and at the Australian embassy. I have until April 30 to decide what to do. If she is not in Australia before this date, her visa will expire or I can cancel it before then.

If I am ever in Thailand, I will look you up so we can have a beer.

Thanks for your advice
Merry Christmas and Happy New Year,
Bruce

***

Scott

Three months later, I emailed Bruce to get an update on his situation.

Hi Bruce,
Just wondering Bruce, whatever happened with your girl?

Scott

***

Bruce

Hi Scott,

Good to hear from you.

After heaps of thinking on what to do I, canceled my wife's visa to come to Australia. Then the embassy called her to tell her the visa has been canceled because we were no longer in a lasting relationship. My wife phoned me every night crying. She plays the victim so well.

I wrote a letter back to the embassy reinstating her visa.

CHOWDERHEAD!

I told her she can come to Australia on the condition she books a return ticket for six months and she pays for her plane ticket. I am not listening to all the advice my friends have given me.

Hey, what have I got to lose?

Time, money and most importantly, self-respect!

It will either work or she will go back after six months. This time I am not so quick on handing out money and have not given her any cash. She no longer has the same wandering eyes. She can work in Australia now, but I think she is really not that interested in working.

Why should she when she can sit on her ass and collect his money!

She can earn much better money here in Australia.

After her six months is up in November, if things go well, I will tell to her I will refund the return plane ticket back to Thailand and she can live here with me. If she still wants to go back to Thailand, then she is not serious about our marriage. Before we got married, we both agreed to live in Australia and return to Thailand for six weeks every year.

She tells me she misses her home and family, but if she goes back to Thailand she wants to go back to work in Phuket, so she will not be living with her family anyway.

Still read your site every week. You have some really good advice.

Anyway thanks again,
Take Care,
Bruce

Final Thoughts

Nice guy… way too nice. He let her get away with far more than he should have. When Bruce first brought her to Australia and she made the statement about only loving him, it was a sign and her way of telling him she's going to do what she wants, like it or not. Instead of drawing a line in the sand and saying, "Hey, that shit doesn't fly with me honey," he got pissed off and basically did nothing.

When she cried, he caved instead of letting her cry. A leopard can't change its spots and I doubt this woman would have stuck around if he had set boundaries in the beginning of the relationship. Some men will put up with anything, either because they view their relationship as strong and don't want to rock the boat, or they are weak, insecure, inexperienced, afraid to be alone or lazy. Whatever his reasons, I think he's going to be miserable for as long as he is with her. Hopefully, they'll prove me wrong.

Charlie - Charlie Is Definitely Not In Charge

Charlie

Dear Scott,

I watch your YouTube videos regularly and I find them to be very informative. Like you, I currently live in Bangkok. I've written with the hopes my letter will either be replied by you or be the basis of one of your videos.

Perhaps something like:

"Living With a Bar Girl: How Do I Escape Her and Move to Another Apartment Without Bloodshed."

I've been living with a very popular bar girl from Sukhumvit Soi 4, Nana Plaza for the past year and a half. She was smitten by my lovemaking prowess as well as my endowment. Her nickname for me is *Hum Yai or* Big Penis. At first, it was a novel experience being with a hot looking bar girl and not paying for sex, but the situation has steadily become untenable these past four months or so. She is uber-jealous and will throw tantrums when I go out with my male friends for a friendly drink.

This is totally unacceptable. If she is jealous at this point of the so-called relationship, it is only going to get worse. Time to give her the boot.

Because of her, I have lost my primary income source. My business is entertainment orientated, and it necessitates that I go to various bars to talk to girls as well as patrons. This is impossible, since I'm under 24/7 surveillance and lockdown. Due to her veteran status, she has operatives everywhere who will report my whereabouts if I leave my room. Once she leaves for her shift at work at 6PM, SkyNet is immediately activated.

This woman is very violent and destructive, especially when she's drunk. She drinks for a living, so this is frequent. It has become a nightly ordeal. I need to escape her, but want to do so without bloodshed— MINE!

What does this say? She's a wack job! Danger Will Robinson, danger!

As a result of my lost income source, I'm at subsistence level where this woman now supports me. I've lost my balls and I now must feverishly reclaim them before it's too late.

I'm planning on moving from my apartment (where she resides with me) this coming August to escape this hell I am in. I have a friend who's moving to Bangkok from the USA and we plan on sharing a 2 bedroom apartment together. My friend and I will be going into business together. The key to doing so is separating me from this woman.

Do you have any words of wisdom you can impart? How I can move away from this psychotic woman without incurring violence to myself? There may be others in a similar situation, so if you read this on your channel as a dedicated subject, maybe others can help.

Thank you for reading my message.

Sincerely,

Charlie NOT in Charge

* * *

Scott

Charlie,
A few questions...

As I sense the urgency, I will give some quick advice and ask a few questions. For now, I'm not even going to go anywhere near some of the mistakes you made.

1. Is the apartment in your name or hers? If it is, you need to get the apartment to stop her from entering. That's the first step.

2. Do you have money to pay her off? Like 100-200K baht. I know this may sound like a helluva lot, but if she's hot, she probably makes a nice chunk of change every month so she's going to expect a decent payoff from you. You always pay, sometimes it's financial, sometimes not, but in the end, the payoff is a common way of quickly eliminating this problem.

3. *If possible, pack your shit while she's at work and move elsewhere. Anywhere else, but do not let her or her operatives know where you are going. This is obviously imperative. Even if you have to shack up in some shit hole guest house for a month, do it.*

If you must stay, remove any sharp items, bottles, etc., basically anything she can use as a weapon. The less possibilities the better, because it sounds like she will act first and think later. When bar girls drink, their issues tend to make them volatile, so you definitely have reason to worry. It might not hurt to go to the Lumpini police station before anything happens, just in case. If the police have a report on file demonstrating your concern and her violent nature, this might help you later on. Believe me; it is worth taking the time to do so. But again, do whatever you have to do to escape. A motorcycle is best—easier to disappear.

If she goes crazy and attacks you with a weapon, do not hesitate to stop her. Grab her, choke her out, knock her out, do whatever is necessary. Self-preservation outweighs everything and while I am not one to advocate violence to solve a problem, she could take an eye out, slice up your face with a bottle, or worse. I have seen this happen several times and almost always, the bar girl is fueled by alcohol and bitterness.

Once you are out, do not see her again. If for some reason you must communicate with her, do so via text. Put as much space between you and her for as long as possible. This means you will need to stop going to the bars, at least temporarily.

I went out with a smoking hot go-go dancer from Nana for a few weeks and she slowly began moving in her stuff; clothes, shoes, shampoo, anything she could. I wasn't paying her and I admit, at first I was nice. She stayed with me every night. Once in a while I paid her bar fine, but I got the distinct feeling she was marking her territory and setting the trap. It just didn't feel right.

I decided to tell her I didn't want to continue seeing her.

"This thing between you and I isn't going to work. You need to get your stuff and take it home."

Short and sweet. She went berserk. Screaming, yelling, getting in my face and calling me every name in the book. Why any woman would go nuts over me is a mystery, but I remained calm, kept my side of the conversation civil and said as little as possible.

After a few minutes, she began picking up her

possessions and stuffing them in her oversized purse, stomped around mumbling to herself. I sat down and turned on the TV, watching her out of the corner of my eye.

A few months later, I ran into one of her friends. She told me the girl understood why I split up with her, but she was happy I finished with her the way I did.

Getting into a shouting match and name calling only makes matters worse; better to downplay the situation and leave the woman with some semblance of dignity. Life is hard enough.

People can be a bit slow to figure out what is truly best for them (or their partner). Your girl may hold a grudge for a bit, but as time passes, she will get over it. They all do, and in most cases, more rapidly than expected.

Just remember, what you need is breathing room to let her get over you and to find someone else. She'll hate you for a while, maybe even forever, but if so, who cares? If she does, she does, if she doesn't, great. But the important thing is to extract yourself with your balls intact and hopefully to be able to make your rounds of the bars without having major problems.

If it makes you feel any better, I have been in the position you are in. I was out of money, unemployed, and had no idea what was next for me. I could barely take care of myself, much less some needy Thai whore. I met a girl at the Beer Garden on Sukhumvit Soi 7. We went out, had a lot of fun together and started spending every second together. By this time though, my bank account was dwindling and the monthly payment I had been receiving for the sale of my business stopped being sent. The buyer was earning less than expected and one day, my payment stopped coming. Instead of going back and fighting for what I was owed, I wrote it off. Then I preserved what little money I had left.

One night, my little friend went out, got drunk, and threw a temper tantrum. She then told me she was leaving because she needed someone with money. As if to make me feel better, she said she would be with me again once I started bringing in some money. I guess she got tired of paying the tab at the bar every night.

It took time, but I got my act together and ran into her again about a year and a half later. When she heard I was back on my feet financially, she said wanted to start seeing me again. I had learned my lesson though. During our time apart, I met Beau, the woman who is now my wife. We were getting serious and although I could have been with either of the two, I knew Beau was the better choice. I had been dumped over a lack of money before and it could certainly happen again.

After our conversation, I left her crying in the rain, because I told her I didn't want her. Cry for me when I have money, leave me when I don't. Bye-bye honey, it's your loss.

Looking back, this was probably one of the best decisions I have ever made in my life.

Good luck and talk to you soon,
Scott

***

Charlie

Hello Scott,

First, I'm appreciative you've taken the time to read my plea. As you surmised, I'm in a precarious and somewhat dangerous position. Yes, time is fast becoming an issue since August will be here before you know it. That's when my USA friend is coming out and we'll be getting a 2 bedroom apartment together.

To respond directly to your questions:

1. The apartment lease is in my name and I am currently on a month to month basis. Regrettably, there is no security here in my building. I live in a dilapidated apartment complex here on Soi 4 Sukhumvit. It is literally a "fun house" inhabited by all sorts of people ranging from retirees to hookers. It is relatively close to the Nana Entertainment Complex. Since there is no security, I have no way of keeping her out. Obviously, my next apartment will have 24/7 security with preferably ID check-in for all women.

2. Your assumption is accurate. I do not have the money to pay her off. I had already paid an amount for recent debts incurred, but that is not germane to your suggestion. I also have heard of cases where guys pay women to get them to leave. Extortion, but sometimes it works. Since I don't have the requisite funding since my income stream was halted, this is not an option.

3. Your suggestion to scramble and pack up all my things and vacate immediately to a cheap hotel certainly has merit. This thought has crossed my mind many times. Regrettably, I'm not at liberty to do this because of my dire financial situation. I'm at subsistence levels right now. I need to just hold out or hide out until my American friend comes in August.

On to your other suggestions:

I have already removed all knives, glass bottles, etc., from the premises. I keep my eyes on any other things which may be used as a weapon. When this woman and I get into our fights, she will always threaten to smash up my computer. This is my main source of communication with the outside world, so I protect like a hockey goalie.

Your suggestion to do a preemptive strike by registering a report with the Thai Police Department in Lumpini is very worthwhile in my opinion. I have this individual's information; her Thai ID number and Thai Passport number. My only concern is whether or not they will notify the girl that I filed a premature report like this. If yes, I don't think it would wise. This will only aggravate her and exacerbate the situation. Perhaps you can shed some light on this as I contemplate it.

If she is truly a mental case and is making his life miserable, Charlie needs to stand up her, tell her the relationship is over and at the very least, have the lock on his door changed. Of course, he won't do this because he wants to use her to support himself. So there is a trade off.

Regarding my resistance to defend myself in the event there is a true violent attack with knives, broken bottles, or whatever, I will not hesitate to put her down. I'm well-versed in martial arts and boxing, but I will only use my skills to restrain. However, if I feel my life is truly threatened, I will knock her out. I'm afraid that a well placed blow could result in serious bodily harm or death. I do not want that on my conscious and that's why I'm looking for a more reasonable way out of my predicament.

Once I have escaped and moved into my new

apartment, I will initiate a zero contact policy with her. I also agree with your suggestion that I should stay away from Soi Nana (where her bar is located) for a cooling off period. This period might be as long as several months. There are plenty of other entertainment venues I can prospect as I resume my income producing business. Soi Cowboy, Patpong, etc.

You stated that you once faced a similar situation with a hot Nana go-go dancer. You say you threw her out. How did you effectuate this without injury? Perhaps the lady you referenced was not as crazy as the one I'm currently with. Obviously, she didn't go voluntarily. Did she cause damage to your personal property on the way out? I don't mean to pry, but I'd like to see if there are any similarities between what you went through and what I'm contemplating.

At this stage of the game, I don't care if she hates me forever. I want to survive and live again. I did not move from the USA to Thailand to be in the proverbial shackles of this lady. I made the mistake of screwing her too well when I was initially with her. 'Mr. Hum Yai' is all she would croon. As I stated in my initial message to you, the novelty of getting free sex with a little nymphomaniac was great. I have been banging her like there was no tomorrow for months on end since she lived with me, but the frequency of sex now is very sporadic, sometimes abstaining for weeks on end. It sucks. Misery and no sex.

This all boils down to control. As this woman senses my friend coming to my rescue, she becomes more chaotic and unstable. The added variable of alcohol really ramps up the danger.

On to your last paragraph regarding the girl who gave you the ultimatum. She dumped you because she was tired of paying the tab, but alerted you that she would you take you back once you started earning again. Please do not misunderstand me. Once I am away from this harpy and start earning again, I don't care if she wants me back or not. I'm looking to make a permanent escape. Yikes!

I firmly believe the subject matter we're discussing is relevant to many of your YouTube and blog audience. I'm suffering greatly from a psychological and spiritual standpoint and I bet there are guys who are in the same boat as me. I appreciate you taking the time to discuss this with me. You've provided me with some very useful advice.

Thanks again for taking time out from your hectic schedule to address my problem.

Warm regards,
Charlie

***

Scott

Charlie,

Can't you borrow $1000 from your family or a friend back in the US? If I were you, I would search high and low for the cash. You might have already done this but this would certainly help you right now.

I'm assuming you are letting her live with you because she's supporting you. Obviously this is important, but you wouldn't be the first guy in this position nor will you be the last.

I think I know the place where you're staying. It's on

the left side of Soi Nana, down a little alley, and on the right side. That little street is a bit of a shit hole.

If you report the girl, I do not believe they will tell her. You can ask them but I'm fairly certain they will not.

The girl I told to pack up and go was crazy too, but once she started getting angry I simply pointed out that if she started giving me any trouble I would dump her on her head outside my door. That was enough. I have thrown out a couple of Thai women, but fortunately I was able to get them out by intimidation more than anything else.

Regarding the girl who dumped me, if you can call it that, we actually had a pretty good relationship and she was very mellow. The first time she left, I was not very happy. But this situation is different from yours and I did not have many serious issues with any of the women.

I once made the mistake of giving a girl a key to my apartment so I could go out and when I came home, she would be there waiting. I forgot all about it. I brought over another girl and we were lying in bed together when the chick with the key came waltzing in.

"Sorry, sorry," she said, immediately turning around and walking out the door. I got out of bed, followed her outside, told her it was no problem and that was enough to get her to come back inside.

Next thing I know, the two girls are talking about where they were from and how long they had lived in Bangkok. That was pretty wild and would probably never happen in the US.

There was a freelancer I took who came close to getting violent. She was known for using Heineken bottles when things didn't go her way.

One day she and I got drunk together. I decided to take her back to my place, we had sex and when she left, of course she asked for money, I paid her the going rate at the time, and she began ordering me to give her more. I knew what I gave her was fair and told her no. She got upset and started looking for a weapon. I opened the door, got in her face, which surprised her a little because I had been completely mellow, and picked her up and put her outside my door. She started to come back inside and I gave her the palm. That was all it took. But I did have to pick her up, as she was screaming and yelling, and throw her ass out. The last thing any man needs is someone threatening him with physical violence in his own home.

You almost always pay one way or another and in the end, there is always something they want.

I took one girl almost 20 years ago, one of the first freebies I ever got here in Thailand, and she was great. Sweet, sexy and she gave me everything I wanted. But…she had a habit of coming over whenever she wanted because we were friends. After a few times, this got irritating not to mention inconvenient. She just felt like she could come and go as she pleased. So her inconveniencing my life was how I paid. I had to deal with her coming over when I had other girls at my place, when I was sleeping, at 4AM, whenever she wanted. A major pain in the ass.

Your story is a perfect example of why men should not get involved whores, no matter how good the sex is or how free it seems!

Anyhow, good luck and lemme know if you need

any further help.

Scott

Final Thoughts
What is the most important Golden Rule?

Do not get seriously involved with a working girl.

Charlie let her move in with him in exchange for free sex. Like it or not, according to her, they were in a relationship. Once he let her to move into his apartment, the relationship took on a different dynamic. Prostitutes are meant to fulfill a man's needs, for a price, whatever they may be. Letting her move in might have seemed like a great idea at the time, but moving a whore in is a helluva lot easier than moving them out.

Bar girls are human, they have feelings, emotions, dreams, they are people, blah, blah, blah. I understand, but the cold, hard truth is that when a woman becomes a prostitute, she is a hired gun. If another guy comes around with a bigger, better deal, she's gone. Men should have their fun with working girls; laugh, joke, talk and when the session is over, smile, say goodbye and go on their way. Charlie's made the mistake of letting a prostitute move in to his apartment in exchange for what he thought was free sex.

He is lucky to have escaped with his balls intact. Hell hath no fury like a whore discarded.

Craig - The Nut Job

Craig

Out of all the people who have written to me, I disliked this guy the most. Looking back, I realize craziness is seldom personal and I just happened to be in his path. Had he clicked on someone else's video instead of mine, I may never have heard from him.

When Greg began emailing me, I was relatively new to YouTube and had no clue how to handle online trolls and people like him.

Experience has taught me the majority of trolls send message for a myriad of reasons; boredom, frustration, loneliness, a lack of direction, misery or perhaps they hate their job or wife or life. Any of these reasons can compel a person to troll in an odd attempt to make them feel better.

Slowly but surely, Craig attempts to persuade, and then pressure me into meeting with him. Even after I informed him I had no intention of meeting with him, he remained undeterred. His determination was slightly unnerving. Finally, I told him I was too busy and if he wanted to meet with me, he should pay a consultation fee. This was the first time I asked someone to pay to meet with me. He disregarded this idea, and then informed me he would pay at some point, all the while continuing to press me to meet with him.

Had I simply ignored his request, he might have gone

away, never to be heard from again. Who knows? His letters started out friendly, and at one point I almost felt sorry for him. That is, until he revealed his true nature. Feeling sorry for him would have been a mistake.

***

Craig

Dear Scott,

My name is Craig and I live in Newcastle on the East coast of Australia. I have been traveling to Thailand since 2003, and like you, I guess I am hooked on the carefree, happy go lucky people, their King and their country.

First paragraph and he assumes to know me and why I am in Thailand. While he is not all together wrong, there are many reasons I like Thailand and several I do not.

I have a Thai wife of ten years and together we have one child who is now four years old. I myself, like you, have had my share of misfortune with me health, which I can elaborate on at another time.

Once again he attempts to inform me how similar the two of us are, and thus we should be friends. I am not opposed to meeting with people, even people I may not particularly like, but from the get-go I had a bad feeling about him.

I consider myself to be unlike everybody else. I tend to test and analyze everything these days, which I actually enjoy doing. This, of course, prevents mistakes. And again, why? Well, Scott, that again, will be another story which I would be happy to try and explain to you, maybe on Sukhumvit Soi 7 at another time, LOL!

Selfishly, I need to meet you, sometime up the track, when it is convenient to you and of course, I. You are a wealth of information, what can I do for you?

I am 55-years-old, work as a communications technician, I can handle earth moving equipment, I can drive a continuous miner in a coal mine and I can polish timber floors extremely well. In other words, we endeavor to always give people a good value for the money and also the highest quality.

Who is we? What on earth does this matter to me?

However, I fucked up Scott and now collect a disability pension. With a bit of luck though, I will be able to come and live my dream in the land of the Thai!

I have a lot of decisions to make in the coming months. First, I would like to communicate with you on Skype, if possible and tell you my plan. Okay?

The truth is I need to know you, but I guess you don't need to know about me, lol.

I am not at all wealthy, but if you require a fee to spend time with me, well then you may mention this, for my consideration.

Actually, you seem like a man of the world and I would like to try and get to know you. Maybe I might bring something into your life that interests you, who knows? However, at this point, we need a little help.

Again, who is we?

I will await an email from you and maybe we can go from there. I will enlighten on my pseudo-handle again another time. It should make you laugh.

Above all, don't think too much. That is all I can say at this point. Thank you.

***

Scott

Hi Craig,

Please enlighten me on the Frank Schmegma handle.

Visiting and living here are two entirely different matters and once you've been here for a while, this becomes much more apparent. Yes, I like the laid back lifestyle and in most cases, the people. There is blatant racism and discrimination, constant political problems and the Thai inability to accept any criticism or consider views beyond their own keeps this country from being as perfect as many thinks. However, most countries have similar negatives.

I do not go to lower Sukhumvit much anymore. I take photos there once in a while, but other than this I have no need or desire to hang out there. I used to live on Sukhumvit Soi 1 and got my fill of the place ten times over. Nowadays, I stick to the Bangkapi area where I live and only go elsewhere if I have a worthwhile reason to do so.

Are you planning on retiring here? How is it I can help you?

I make videos to entertain while at the same time generating a little revenue. Most people who write me want something from me and there's not much in it for me. Like you said, and most of the time this is the case, you need to know me, I don't really need to know about you.

So here's the deal: I would be happy to help you, but I charge for consultations. My rate is $25 for a 30 minute consultation and $45 for an hour consultation, payable through PayPal. If you require me to come to you, travel time is an additional two hours.

Regards,
Scott

***

Craig

Thanks Scott! Glad to actually get a personal post from you!

I fully understand what you are doing and as far as I am concerned, it is well received, blatantly honest from my perspective!

I figure I'm about six month away from moving to Thailand. Put it this way, I have a four-year-old, half-Thai boy who has to start school in 2015. So...it's now or never.

It will happen, as I have a life to live and I'm on my final run to meet my maker. I want to do so on my own terms. I have worked all my life and have had enough of serving others. Just once I want to serve myself.

My story is long and it should amuse you a little, however, I am proud of my miserable achievements, no matter how insignificant anyone else might view them.

Look, you get many offers of friendship, I am sure, but if you are not fully over the human race, kindly consider meeting with me on my next arrival. I think when living as an expat in a foreign land, it is good to have friends or perhaps acquaintances. I don't fancy a totally reclusive life and I have measured you as analytical, similar in some ways as a writer.

Craig seemed to be a bit out there to me, but at this point I had no problem with him and figured being polite and direct with him was the best approach. Some

people visiting Thailand erroneously seem to think I have no life and have all the time in the world to meet with them. When Craig asked me to meet with him, I did not want to meet with him. I had things to do that I valued far more than a meeting with a guy I don't know and who I found strange. Paying for my time was the only way I would meet with him.

I will endeavor to send you a Christmas present before Christmas. As long as I keep my customers happy, I expect to have my palm greased (in a manner of speaking). In turn, I will remember you and accordingly plan to grease your palm. Just a little sweetener so that you may spare me a thought.

I have no fucking idea what I am going to do (in Thailand) to wile the time away, but mind you, I will only have to please myself. No more undeserving customers, no more mail boxes, limited people speaking my language and finally, I can limit the amount of adversity that I may have to endure, lol.

I think sharing a meal on Soi 7 or maybe a meal wherever you feel is a good place would be a good start. You can bring your wife and kids, no problem; I'll cough up the cost, happily, and entertain you! Now, one last thing, please give me a little room, remembering that I am only Australian.

"Remembering that I am only an Australian?" What on earth does this mean?

I have no problem buying meals for myself and my family. How many doctors, lawyers, financial consultants or psychiatrists offer their services for a meal at The Beergarden?

What he didn't get, and many people do not, is that

time is money and time is a limited resource. If I give my time, there needs to be a reason; friendship, information, or money. If I'm giving up my time to someone like Craig, the only reason is money. I give my advice and in return, I expect financial compensation. I don't want coffee, lunch, dinner, or a box of chocolates. Despite what he had previously told me, he was unwilling to pay a fee.

Ask me any question you wish to know, I am only too happy to accommodate.

Presently my wife and I, with the help of a couple of lazy sons, have been rebuilding an old bus depot. I think you Americans would call it a bus station.

Considering I have been cleaned out by 2.5 ex-spouses, we are not doing too badly. Usually most would have succumbed to the inevitable nightmare of bankruptcy, but Scott, it seems I have slipped through the net and escaped getting my face rubbed in shit. It seems I have made it to the other side! And rightly so, I have worked my guts out in the past. I am unsure whether we rent the property or just sell it. My only fear is if I fall on the most unthinkable condition, like a heart attack or some other insidious situation that reminds me of my fallible being. I would like to think that I could crawl onto a 747 and hightail it back to the Land of Oz to try and get repaired. Owing to my understanding of the Thai economy, I feel things in Thailand are no longer cheap and getting heart surgery in Thailand would bankrupt me. I don't want to think too much of these things. I think I would like to fall off the twig in Thailand and may my bones bleach in the tropical sun.

So Scott, there is some small enlightenment for you

to consider. I hope to meet with you before I am no more.

Sincerely,
Craig

P.S. Here is my phone number XXXXXXXXXXX. Only if you're feeling lonely, lol.

I now think this guy is on the drink and a nut job.

***

Scott

I am still unsure of what you're after, but if you want to meet with me, please pay the consultation fee. It's as simple as that.

***

Craig

Look, I've looked at your work and have seen how you deliver yourself. What I have taken note of is you are thorough. I hope you are appreciated by the masses. I said to you before, that generally speaking, people don't take kindly to the truth. It always has to be colored so that the deliverer of the truth is respected and safe. However, you're doing it and you seem to be getting away with it. On a personal note, I understand and like what you do. I am not patronizing you, however at the rate you are producing this work, and I have a hunch that eventually there will be knockers. In the end, this is life.

I don't want anything from you. I simply see a guy that is educated and obviously bit the bullet a long time ago and moved to the land of the Thai. For what it is worth, I commend you on your success. You have lived in Thailand for a long time as well, of course, at a disadvantage.

I have observed how Thais set it up. I feel we are The Dole Office of Thailand (Free money, free soup kitchen) and Thais enjoy gouging *farang,* lol. The Thais are smart and we will never be Thai. Sadly, they won't let us be. We will always be the underclass. But you Scott are still alive. The Thais haven't killed you yet and I am amazed!

I am sitting down here and you're sitting up there. Needless to say, I am pissed off about that. In my spare time, in the afternoons, I send An American in Bangkok messages, a guy who is living my dream!

In the end, I have to be self-funded. I really can't do it any other way. If I sold up everything that I own, maybe I could get my hands on AUD$700,000. Yeah, a reasonable amount of money, for sure, but considering what I have done and how I did it through the years I have been headily dispossessed. I should be worth millions, but this greedy litigation system, along with the wants and needs of women (which is how the silver tails make their money - it's their legal profession), have taken much from me. However, I am not the only one!

Craig has lost the plot and has decided to give me far more information than I want or need. In recent times I have turned the tables back on them and managed to get myself classified as a dimwit. In turn, the do-gooders have given me a pension, which I hope I can take to Thailand soon. The rules in this regard means I have to be classified as totally incapacitated, which is what I am waiting on. You see, here in Australia, if you pay your taxes and you get lucky, it is possible for one to get their hands on the free lunch, in a matter of speaking.

So in other words, when I get this commercial

property completed, I don't have to sell it. I can live in The Garden of Eden and suck an orange at the government's expense. Is this not the right thing to do? I am sure you are a Republican, lol.

Craig is rambling on and on and I am starting to wonder if he is drunk or on drugs or has some sort of brain damage or mental illness. Whatever his issue is, he is very strange, to put it mildly.

I have been screwed, so now I have a bad attitude. Call it war—me against them!

So wrapping up, this time around I will show you my heart and endeavor to grease your palm. I am hoping you will agree to spend some time with me and my happy little family and maybe break bread together. That's all mate, I don't want your money or your blood, just a bit of company with the smarts. You're one of them. I'm smart Scott, because I have recognized you as smart. As I have said before, my story is long and interesting by anyone's measure. I have had enough, I want out!

You know how to organize, how to get good, fair priced accommodations, you know where to buy things for survival, you know, you know! Maybe over time we can entertain each other. One can only hope! Of course, we could all appropriate the predictable human behavior and think too much. Let's hope not! You have nothing to fear knowing me!

The only fear I have is accidentally meeting this guy. The more he writes, the more out there I think he is and I have no intention of meeting him.

Last, just for you, my handle Frank Schmegma. Okay, I will answer your question! A long, long time ago, I had a job in telecommunications, working as a technician. Back then, Australia's public utilities were federally owned. This was a good thing for the people owned the assets!

I left this safe government job and started my own private communications company. I was one of the first to do so in this country. Your country was already long established into private enterprise. Please remember, you have 360 million people, we have 23 million. Big difference!

Okay, at the time, I had lots of long-standing friends still on the job. I would regularly telephone what was known as the test desk. The guy answering would ask who was speaking and I would always answer, "Frank Schmegma." So next I would hear this name being spewed out over the public address, lol. For example, 'Joe Tierney, Frank Schmegma on line seven, call for you.' I would always laugh out loud.

Let us quantify this, shall we?

Frank = honest, straight forward, outspoken, blunt, inherently honest (sounds like you Scott).

Schmegma = a buildup of skin and other crud found between the foreskin and penis.

This is my observation of general humanity, based historically. Human history? Appalling!

So there you have it. Please write back, I will respond.

Note: the next post will be my reasons for wanting to get out there. They are the exact same reasons you don't want to return to The Big Apple!

I look forward to meeting you Scott!

After a rambling message like this, who in their right mind would want to meet with this guy? Craig is

71

like a little girl asking a boy to be her boyfriend—on their first date. I don't know this guy, these are his first emails to me, and while he may think he knows everything about me, I know enough about him that I don't want to meet with him unless he forks over the cash.

***

Scott

If you want a paid consultation, let me know.

All the best,
Scott

***

Craig

Look Scott! This is difficult. The written word is not the way to really, truly present one's self. Maybe one of the parties wishes to form a relationship of sorts.

I actually type at a 100 miles per hour, so to write some paragraphs to endeavor to enlighten you can be done very swiftly.

Look! I got the shits, okay? I just want to get out of the place. I probably don't like my civil liberties being revoked, because the people who revoked them feel they're more qualified than me to make such a call on my behalf. I probably don't like all these ruling classes who do absolutely nothing for the GNP of this stupid land.

Maybe I don't like the way the place turned out! I have also been robbed by the people I trusted. Look, we can talk about this over coffee, if you would let your guard down. I don't want anything from you, okay?

Yes, he does, he wants my time and this is more than I am willing to give.

I decided to like you because you laid it all on the line. The things you have talked about rang my bell! I want nothing, got it?

However, I would like to be a friend to you! I have quite a few friends already in Thailand. Just one guy I bring to mind is Don down in Phuket. He actually is a Pommy. He resided in Australia for around thirty years, has a pension and has lived there in Thailand for fifteen years. He is an old guy and I like him as well. I have known him for around ten years. At present he is in a bit of trouble. Apparently the teller machine has sucked his F-Pos Card in and swallowed it. He comes from West Australia, which equates to you like California or New York—similar geographic.

I have a stock broker friend who just so happens to be traveling to Thailand very soon to see his pregnant wife, lol. Don is getting a new card sent to my address and I will forward it on through to Ian, my mate, through the post office in Bangkok in an effort to speed things along for old Don. He needs his F-Pos Card in quick time. Everything has to fall in place though, otherwise I will be sending it from here priority snail mail. Don has nobody except me, or so it would seem. I am happy I rank high enough for him to choose me to help him out.

Am I the only one who thinks Craig is a drama queen? Everything seems to be a big deal, everyone is out to get him and he is way too caught up in telling his story. Mind you, this is a story I would rather not read.

Now, getting back to you and me. I am trying to get you to let your guard down and let me into your world (just a little). You know, you are English speaking, and your General MacArthur saved all these non-deserving Australians that now reside here in 2013. Much American blood was shed in an effort for you and me and others to walk free. Having said that, you were brought up in a country of 350 million and that accounts for you being careful. You have probably been burned as well, like all of us.

Nope, I can't say that I have ever been seriously burned. Maybe it has to do with me being cautious about who I allow into my inner circle. Craig is someone my inner circle can do without.

I actually have large gates up on my property to keep the hangers on out. As I live in a city equating to every man and his dog whom feel they are my friend, and just decided to drop in and generally give me the shits and waste my time whenever they feel they want to. I have locked them out so you better consider yourself lucky I decided to like you! Please do not let your ego get in the way of that smart comment; you can handle it, lol. Only guys like Scott Mallon would rank as one that I would like to mix it up with a little. Let's see how you handle that!

Craig

Lucky? That's the last thing I was feeling when I read this message. I really wanted to try and remain detached and unemotional as possible with this guy. After re-reading his letters, it is clear he is a head case.

***

Scott

Okay, what are your reasons for leaving Oz. And please, keep it short.

***

Craig

I fully understand you and you are respected. Hopefully we can exchange thoughts when time allows. Actually I want to grease your palm a little. Heck, that's what makes the world go round, but give me a little more time on that one, as we are on the Christmas rush and the money has to be dragged in! I won't forget and I am a man of my word. My word is iron!

I have a Facebook site and have many followers. I have been a little laid back on the rhetoric lately, so I will just ask you to scroll down a little more and friend me to get a look at the lot. Anyhow, no matter.

My gorgeous Thai wife of ten years has just summoned me to pick her up in the car. It is with great pleasure to know you. I ask that we just take it as it comes. I understand you! And cut the one liners, I don't carry a gun, okay?

Thanks,
Frank Schmegma.

P.S. I actually do not like the social aspect of this medium called Facebook, but I succumbed, injecting a little disrespect into all this pissing in each other's pocket stuff called Facebook. Lol, once again!

***

Scott

Craig,

My one liner wasn't meant in a negative fashion. Perhaps you should slow your thoughts and typing. I also can type quickly, but I am calculating and thus, think before typing.

I am not sure what in the world you're talking about when referring to my ego. I have no greater or lesser ego than any other man. Frankly, my questioning why you want to leave Australia was just that, a question.

Understand something. I do not know you and you do not know me. I trust very few people and I do not allow myself to be pushed into trusting anyone or become friends with them—ever. No offense, but please stop trying to get me to let my guard down and let you into my world. It's not going to happen—ever. This is me. I have a family here and in the United States and a circle of friends I have known for many years. I do not try to make friends or easily allow people into my world. That's laying it all out there for you.

I said I would meet with you for a fee. My time is my time and I do what I want with it. This is why I set up my life here in Thailand the way I did. If I met and exchanged emails with everyone who wanted to meet with me or speak with me I would never have any time for myself. This is why I told you I charge people a consultation fee. There are far too many people who think if they buy me coffee or throw me ten dollars I will talk to them for hours on Skype or in person. Look at it from my perspective: Ten dollars for an hour-long taxi ride to meet, then another couple of hours to let them pick my brain over lunch or dinner (which I am capable of buying myself) and then another hour to get home. This is never going to happen. Never.

So my attitude towards you is nothing personal.

Hopefully you will understand where I'm coming from.

Scott

***

Craig

Hi Scott,

This is Craig from Australia.

Listen, I have been needling you about chatting. I guess, respectfully, I probably wanted to get to know you. My only reasons were I love Thailand, I love the freedom and the biggest reason is because you are a survivor and as well as this, I could see me and you chatting and probably enjoying each other's company. Well, that was my dream!

You have a lot going on. From your perspective, you probably have enough friends. In my time walking on the surface of the planet earth, I have figured out just what's going on here, lol.

Look, as much as I would like to get to know you, truthfully, you probably don't need me hassling you to piss in my pocket. Look, I don't know how to deliver this, actually I just started it. I am the one with the anxiety. I am the one that wishes to live in Thailand. Your videos are blatantly honest and I like them a lot. But presently, you have a job to do. I will leave you alone, you are a busy man.

Please don't respond. I will be satisfied with just watching your videos and suffering here in Australia with my ball and chain strapped to my ankle (not referring to my gorgeous wife).

So…wrapping up, just forgive me. Just leave it at that.

Sincerely,
Craig

P.S. Oh that comment about the word ego wasn't meant to be taken the wrong way. It was meant as a joke. See how dangerous the written word is? Based on historical human behavior, it's scary! We have to choose our words very carefully when communicating this way. I am happy to communicate this way, however. If you are not sure about anything, just be patient and ask the question, I will gladly explain in detail if required!

Thank you,

Craig

I did not respond. I had hoped he was finished sending me his long, rambling messages, but I was wrong.

Craig

Just in case you are wondering, I agree with your response, however, you and I are probably affected by street level Thais. As you are aware, they generally give us hell on a daily basis. It kind of wears you down after a while.

I have no idea where he got this idea. While irritating situations arise every so often, saying Thais give me hell on a daily basis is jumping to a conclusion based on his experiences, not mine, and he lives in Australia, not Thailand!

There's another guy living there that gets on YouTube and does his blurb. He is a bit of a tough American like you. He has had Thailand up to his neck, seems he can't take it anymore, lol.

Reading between the lines, I think he is stuck

because he may have visa problems for his family getting into the US. He was bitching resoundingly a few months back; however I see he is still in Thailand. I was surprised. If I were to send him that blurb, he might neck himself, lol.

Again, no idea what this guy is talking about. Personally, I think I will probably always live in Thailand at least a few months out of each year for no other reason than it is a good place to live, my wife and children were born here and this is their home. Moving anywhere permanently, even part-time, means additional expenses and until my family is at the point financially where we can live in multiple locations without it stressing our bank account, we will continue living in Thailand. Craig seems to have a penchant for assuming he knows what is what, and the truth is, this other guy on YouTube he is referring to might just have been letting off steam. He does not know.

Anyhow, I am still coming, probably in February or March depending on ticket prices. The down side of life in the fast lane is that it is hard to maintain and it is hard to jump off. Over all it's expensive. If I continue to maintain my life here, I will eventually cave in to a heart attack. So like I have said, there are problems everywhere you are and you go.

Living in Thailand will be a reality for me soon enough. I am armed to the back teeth. All I can hope for is luck! I have many horrific stories involving *farang* having to deal with moral atrocities involving the Thai! But this is the down side. I have to be cunning enough to operate my life quietly, under the nose of the Thai, endeavoring not to poke my head up!

I am actually thinking of paying off my wife and sending her to Isaan to build a dream house for her! Although she has been an absolute gem of a wife, she inevitably weighs me down in my quest for peace and happiness!

Wrapping up, I got what I wanted and ten years later, I question what I have gone and done. The moral issue is this...we have a gorgeous son together. The wrap could be said I am running out on him, but I would probably reside in Phuket and make pilgrimages to Isaan to see him once in a while. No, I am not thinking I can have many Thai women as I am really not interested.

I just hanker for a quiet life. In actual fact, it probably will not happen, but I nurse the thought. My family takes up much of my time and all my sons simply bite chunks out of me. It is all caused by my need to lie on top of women in my early years. God I wish back then I had the fifties wisdom I nurture today!

I made you a promise a few months ago. I intend to grease your palm, but I want to meet you in person, lol. Sorry, that's how it is going to go! I need a dose of you (selfishly).

So we will meet somewhere when I make my landfall, okay? You can set the place and time. I am easy! We will talk, shake hands, eat food and see where it goes. You're paying for the food, lol. I am thinking of relinquishing 7-9 thousand baht to you, to help you and your family, not a big deal, but better than zero. I am only a working class piece of crap myself. I battle to survive in actual fact, but when I come up this time, all our bills are to be paid so I can rest easy and not worry when I get there.

I am the Jack of living here. I want to go some place where nobody knows me, only a chosen few! Think yourself lucky! You have inspired me and I see you as a very interesting character. You are a hard working go-getter, striking hard for his family. Maybe I got it all wrong? Lol, once again. Anyhow, I am not spending this time to set this post out sympathetically for the ease of the reader, you can hopefully figure out what I am endeavoring to tell you!

This guy is a nut job. And yet, for some reason, I wrote him back. Perhaps it was because this was when I had very few subscribers and I wanted all the viewers to think that their messages would be answered. Looking back, I should have completely ignored him and never responded.

***

Scott

Craig,

I should make things a bit more clearly on how I think. You seem to assume you know me. You don't. First, I am rarely affected by Thais on the street. I speak Thai and have no problem dealing with them. They don't give me hell and if any Thais say anything that irritates me, it is usually in a tourist area. Once I speak to them in Thai, there are rarely any serious problems. So I don't catch hell from Thais.

Like I told you before, my time is my time. I make my friends with who I want, when I want, and unless I consider a person my friend, I don't give my time for free. Magazines will often ask to use the written word or photographs for exposure. I don't buy into this.

In other words, if you want something from me, whether it's to meet me and pick my brain or you just need my time, I need to be paid prior to meeting with you. Sorry, but this is how it is going to go. As you said, you need a dose of me, no offense, but I can do without a dose of you.

While you have me right as a go-getter who works hard for his family, I have no idea what you endeavor to tell me.

All the best,
Scott

***

Craig

Thanks for replying. I must say, a bit cold from my perspective, but it is truly a free choice and I must respect that. So based on your last post, it seems the only way you are going to entertain me is via YouTube! Okay, okay, you have told me. I feel a bit awkward about asking you for an audience. Actually, that's all I wanted I guess. It's true, you amuse me!

I am sorry to bother you!

***

Craig

Look Scott, at the end of the day, you are okay! You are giving it your best actually! Okay, so you have to get your hands on legal tender, understood. Guess what, so do I! You know this miserable trip to Thailand that once again I undertake is difficult for me. The bullshit I have to take care so The Man leads me alone is simply unreasonable!

Despite paying at least 1000-2000 dollars to visit Thailand, he is either unable or unwilling to pay for a consultation. This always strikes me as a bit odd. Looking back at his messages, I should have simply sent them all in the trash bin.

I badly want to get the fuck out of here! I am not coming to pick your brain, okay? I don't know, I said I just want to be your friend, that's all!

I know you don't need any friends, lol.

Look, we can meet informally, spend a bit of time together, but maybe you don't want to do this. Well, I am sad. What else can I say?

You know in Queensland, today the arsehole who runs the place has bunged on. A fine, yes, and another fine for leaving your vehicle windows down more than two inches. There is zero tolerance on speed limits. It is not good here Scott! I have to get the hell out of here. I am engineering and working on it. I have friends who feel the same. What's worse, the madness of Thailand or modern Western society?

Well, I'll take my chances in Thailand after what I have had to deal with here!

I have a very good property here and I am lucky to have it, considering I could have been processed by the ladies a couple of times! I am waiting on a claim from an insurance company and also a small process from the government. Then I have to sell this property. I am expecting this to happen in the next couple of months. I have a guy who has been trying to get the place for a year now and he now says he will sign a contract at the end of January. So we will see where it goes. I just want some peace! This is not the free-spirited world I was brought up in! It has become totally ruthless! You coming from Miami, I guess you would understand the word ruthless. There are no points for losing!

I don't know, I tell you all this stuff because I am ugly honest. I want the same back!

I am pissed off with the way things turned out for me in the end and I want out!

Look, if I keep telling you stuff, there will be nothing to talk about at this God-forsaken meeting we may have!

Craig

***

Scott

Craig,

You call my response cold; the truth is I am direct. Don't take it personally. What you expect from me is for me to meet with you. I have told you numerous times and I will not say it again, if you wish to meet with me, pay the consultation fee. And just so we're clear, I look at things quite a bit differently than you do. You are not greasing my palm; you are paying for my time and experienced advice.

You also say you want to meet me for selfish reasons. You want to meet me and if I meet with you, I need payment in return. I have a family and a circle of friends I have known for many years and I don't know you from Adam aside from your long, drawn out, rambling emails. If I help people in person, spend my time and money to meet with them, or spend my time talking to them about whatever it is they want to talk about, or if they want to pick my brain, then it is fair to expect to be paid. Hopefully this is clear enough for you to comprehend. To me, it's simply business. You want my time and time is money.

Sorry if you do not understand this, but I have tried to tell you this as directly as possible and you just don't seem to get it. Why should I be your audience? I have a life and I am busy doing what I want to do. My being on YouTube does not predicate a need or desire to meet with everyone when they come to Thailand. Every day I have people asking me to meet or speak with them when they come to Thailand. If I gave all my time away for free, then where would I be?

All the best,
Scott

***

Craig

Okay Scott, because I want to be your friend so, so much, I have sent you a link! It is extremely entertaining! It's a good old boy, hay seed, playing a guitar! I actually like it; however it's very, very American, LOL a lot! Click on the link and shut up! I meant, enjoy.

Craig

***

Scott

Whether joking or not, telling a person to shut up is one of the worst ways to get them to meet and assist you. This time, I did not respond to his email. However, a month later, he found a reason to email me again.

I had uploaded a video to YouTube about Thai bar girls. As I have said many times, I do not fault anyone for trying to make a buck, especially when it comes to women selling their body. However, I do think it's foolish for a man visiting Thailand, or a new expat to try and turn a whore into a housewife. Most men would never think about making a working prostitute their wife in their own country, so what is different in Thailand?

In fact, there are additional issues. If you plan on marrying a Thai prostitute, chances are her culture is much different from yours. If she has yet to master the English language and a man has yet to learn even basic Thai, there is the language barrier. Money issues and the inability to communication effectively are probably the two leading factors in divorces between Westerners and Thai women. A successful marriage takes work and patience, among other things. Add in the cultural difference, language barrier, and the fact that she is a prostitute, and marriage is a long shot at best. If a man is intent on making a marriage work with a bar girl, they both better be on the same page and have the ability to trust one another.

Time and time again I have seen men come to Thailand on a short holiday, and in a matter of day, they are head over heels in love with a prostitute. Desperate to make the woman his own, he decides marriage is the answer.

Inevitably, problems arise even before ands back in his country. The girl he now views as his future wife may have numerous men taking care of her financially and all of them might also be in love with her. She's just milking each cow for as long as she can, hanging on until one of the men decides to give her as much money as she wants. Then they get married and live happily ever after.

The truth is, once married, they get to know one another, and all of the truths they held back quickly come to light, the relationship usually fails. Some relationships with prostitutes work, but most do not. Would any friend in their right mind recommend a man travel halfway around the world to a Thai brothel to find their future wife and mother of their children?

***

Craig

You pig! I hope to meet a reasonable American one day in my travels! Reasonable, you are not! My ex-wife is a former bar girl and she is the best woman I have ever known! Now, I'm going to bed. I'll save you a seat in hell. It's the least I can do for you!

Wait a minute, now she's his ex-wife?

***

Scott

You are allowed to think and feel how you want Craig. Personally, I think you're a nut case.

***

Craig

Scott, I am an atheist! You are a very unpleasant man! I have studied you, like I said to you! You have gall! You have degenerated your website into a personalized matchmaking site! You may as well wade in the sewer!

Goodbye!

P.S. I am honest Scott. Obviously you do not appreciate it. I can assure you your arrogance and disrespect would not be tolerated face-to-face. Nut case, I am not!

Just let it ride. You deal with dimwits actually asking you how to attract and handle Thai women. Has it come to that? You're just lapping it up; your face gets red when you're pushing the shit out of your face. Maybe you should stop and take a glass of water to cool you down! Like you're the expert, whatever you say goes! Nobody else point of view is tolerated. You are just an ugly, unpleasant son of a bitch, sadly. You beg for money in Bangkok, ha!

First up, I didn't think you were this person, but you definitely are! Like I said, you have gall! I can also tell you would have been reasonably unpopular by your ugly demeanor! I thought you were okay in the beginning, but you failed!

Look, we can do this all night! Just forget it, you just spat arrows, I have spat mine! Let's see how long you last doing what you're doing!

And there's nothing wrong with testing the water in an effort to make friends you sick son of a bitch. Some rarely are like you, some are somewhat near normal.

I have many friends in Thailand! I get emails from them every night! They are normal Scotty! Best of luck!

***

Scott

Buddy, just what is your problem? I told you up front I speak my mind and I am a straight shooter. I didn't appreciate you pushing me to meet with you or befriend you and I really don't care what you think about me. You are a whack job.

I make videos and the vast majority of people agree with what I say in them. If they don't, and you don't, that's fine, we don't have to agree! If this makes me an asshole, so be it! I do what I want, when I want, and meeting with you is the last thing I want to do. Time is money and I'm not about to waste either of them on you. So go to bed, get some sleep and get the fuck out of my life. Thanks in advance.

***

Craig

You are a fat cunt with a very big mouth. You are the reason the world has an evil history! You better shut up. You and those suck holes that follow you are obviously unattached and desperate.

I am sticking up for the 80% of Isaan girls forced by poverty into working at a bar, usually supporting a kid back on the farm! They are true blue, unlike you!

All the women here where I live are ex-bar girls, you fool! They are most exemplary and immigration loves them! They are generally reliable and hard working! You are a fucking cunt Scott. How can you justify the shit that flows out of you? And how do you get away with it? Fuck off and take your ugliness with you! You can't help yourself! STOP!

Final Thoughts

After the first or second email, I should not have responded to Craig. I should have gone with my gut instinct, which was that something was wrong with him. Craig's emails were one of the first set of emails I received from anyone related to my YouTube channel. I had received one or two emails from several different people, most of which asked basic questions about Thailand or if I would like to meet with them, but none like his.

It was around this time when the number of people emailing me increased dramatically. It got to the point where answering all my emails took an hour or two every day. More and more people began asking to meet. In one way, I was honored, in another, I realized meeting with everyone who wanted to do so would take a large portion of my time. While it's nice to help someone in need, time is a precious commodity and one I am unwilling to give freely. One of the most common phrases used by these people, a phrase I grew to hate, was "I just want to pick your brain."

Craig's emails came several times a week for two months. I could have ignored him, and in hindsight, I definitely should have. I could have flat out said no to meeting him, but I didn't. Instead, I asked to be compensated for my time. I see nothing wrong with this approach, but once he made it clear he had no intention of paying for my time, I should have stopped responding to his emails. I didn't though. Lesson learned. It would be the first of many to come. Craig did not write me again—thankfully—and from the information I gathered from his website, he is still living in Australia.

Danny - I'll Bust My Ass to Stay in Thailand

Danny

Dear Scott,
I've been to Bangkok five times, just to see a friend, and I love it there. I want to move there and find a job. I'm 50 and don't have a degree. Can I find a job? I don't care about making lots of money. Thank you.

***

Scott

Honestly, it is highly doubtful.

***

Danny

Is it possible if I work my ass off? I could find a job here in Canada. I work as a manager in a store. Do you think I can find a manager job in Bangkok if work my ass off trying? Thank you.

It would really be great full if you can send me a little list of jobs I can find. How did you get start working in Thailand?

***

Scott

A Thai can be a manager, work less than you work,

91

and he will get the job, not you. You cannot work a job that a Thai can do, which limits your options. Just because you want to work here does not mean Thais want you to and unless you figure out how to support yourself, without a degree your options remain very limited.

At this point, I directed him Ministry of Labor's Prohibited Jobs List

***

Danny

I would just like to know is it possible for me to find work there and is there a company that can help me? Thank you, Scott. Thank you for your help.

I ignored this message as I felt I had given him enough assistance and he needs to do some research for himself.

***

Danny

I hope I can find a job in Bangkok. Are there any companies in Bangkok that can help me find a job or I do I have to do it on my own? Can you help me or suggest where to look for help? Thank you very much. I really need the help Scott. I'm sorry for asking so many questions. Can I work on my girlfriend's family farm?

It is at this point this guy is starting to irritate me. He just doesn't get it. It doesn't take a rocket scientist to understand what I'm telling him. It's one thing to give an answer or two to someone and send them on their way. I'm not one to hold a person's hand though. Nobody did this for me and I made it 20-plus years, and he is no different from me.

Scott is it possible for me to find work? I love to tell my girlfriend who lives on a farm. Is it possible to find work there? I would like to know if I can work at her family farm. Will they let me? Thank you,

Danny

***

Scott

You are not hearing me.

***

Danny

What do you mean not hearing you? I would just like to know if it is possible to find a job there. Can I work on my friend's farm? I thank you so much. Is it possible for you to help me?

Thank you so very much Scott

Starting to see a trend? I don't think this guy has a brain between his ears.

***

Scott

No degree = very limited jobs.
Farming is not allowed.
You either make your own source of income, which you can prove to the Thai government or like I said, it is highly unlikely you will find a job without specialized skills.

I hope I made myself clear.

Scott

***

Danny

Thank you Scott. You made yourself clear. With the skills I have I hope I find a job. Thank you so much for your help. Hope to see you in Bangkok so I can buy you a beer.

Seems as if he is a nice guy, but there isn't a chance in hell I'll meet with him. I do not have the patience to deal with someone like this.

So where in Bangkok do you live Scott?

***

Scott

Bangkapi.

***

Danny

Thank you. Hope you have a nice day. Take care.

Final Thoughts

All the spelling and grammatical errors in his letter have been cleaned up. In some of his letters, the spelling and grammar were so atrocious they were difficult to understand. Danny used no punctuation, there were spelling errors every other word, and to make matters worse, he tried shortening his letters by abbreviating words. He is Canadian, has no degree and his written English skills are terrible. If you were in charge of hiring, would you hire him? I definitely wouldn't.

When it comes to living and working in Thailand, Danny might want to remember the old adage, "Work smart, not hard." While there is something to be said for working hard, if you are an expat living in Thailand, you better know how to work smart.

Young, strong, Thai men and women are willing just as hard as foreigners, if not harder, and for much less. Hard working Thais are a dime a dozen and they are more than willing to bust their asses for a living.

Davey - Just Keep That Wallet Out!

Davey

Hey Scott,

I watched one of your latest videos where you are issuing a general warning regarding falling for a bar girl. That subject hit home with me. Unfortunately I had to learn the hard way. After all, everybody believes, "This time the situation is different."

Wise men know it takes time to figure out if a woman is different, and in the case of bar girls, they are seldom different.

My story...I met this lady in Bangkok one night and we hit it off. I was only going to spend the night with her, but the next morning she hung out and we went for coffee and breakfast. I'm thinking to myself, *Okay, it is probably time for you to go now,* but she wanted to hang out with me for the day and show me around Bangkok.

Not to jump the gun, but he made it easy for her. While her showing him around Bangkok sounds sweet, what about his plans?

Okay, so we hung out together. I had previously booked a four or five day trip to Phuket, so I asked her to join me there, and of course, she was more than willing.

Why would he take a whore to a whorehouse? Oops, I forgot, his situation is different. His girl is different.

We spent the time in Phuket and yes, I had a good

time, and yes, I too thought *Wow, this lady is interesting, etc*. However, she was already prepping me for her expectations, talking about making her family's house like new again and about *sin sod*. It was almost like a business negotiation back and forth. The vacation was over shortly afterwards and back to Bangkok we go, as I have to catch a plane home. Of course, I had to settle up with her before I left and she was quite forward about what she wanted. Plus, she told me she couldn't go back to her job because she stopped working to go with me.

He did not ask her quit her job, so guess what, it's her problem!

I got home and made the mistake of continuing this relationship. Well, as luck would have it, I had an opportunity to go back a couple of months later. I arrive in Thailand and flew back to Udon Thani where I was picked up by her and her family and we went to her house. Of course, her parents and family members were happy to meet me, just keep that wallet out. Anyway, by this time I have applied for a visa for her to come to the states.

Dave's failures to take responsibility for his actions are getting on my nerves. He could and should have nipped this so-called relationship in the bud, but instead kept rolling along.

So, as I get to know this woman, I notice a few things that bother me. She never has anything to say to me, yet she talks to other people plenty. She is highly possessive and suspicious with regard to me.

I tell her that I can't see living like this long term and she says she will stop. Yeah, right.

She gets approved for the visa, but by this time I am

really having second thoughts about the whole mess.

It's about time!

I try dumping her and almost end up stabbed in my hotel room. Being a foreigner in their country, I figure my chances of explaining this to someone and having them actually believe me are about zero. I abandon my attempt to dump her and think well maybe if she comes to the US and sees how my life is she will finally realize I am not a woman chaser.

Davey is a Chowderhead. Had he even the tiniest set of balls, he might have stood up to her, told her to get lost, or thrown her out on her head. Instead, he's going on and on with a woman who is willing to kill him if he breaks off their relationship. It must be love.

Well, after being here for several months, it is obvious this is never going to work. So I am not sure how I did it, but I was able to talk her into going home. Now I just have her bugging the hell out of me, telling me she will wait for me forever...yeah sure you will. She is now living in Pattaya Beach, working in a hotel.

Anyway, I spent at least 10,000 dollars all together on this woman. I have nothing to show for it except some old photos and a pile of paperwork but, I learned a valuable lesson and I am glad it didn't cost me more. It easily could have.

Keep up the good work with the videos.

Regards,
Davey

***

Final Thoughts

In all the years I have lived in Thailand, I have never heard of the police coming to the defense of a prostitute unless it was justified. Many tourists worry about this, but the truth is most Thai police are unwilling to deal with these sorts of squabbles unless serious and absolutely necessary. Thai whores make these threats because they know most foreigners lack the knowledge to call them on their bluff and are scared of going to jail or having to make a payoff. Ten grand is peanuts compared to what it could have cost him. Had he went all in, the relationship could have cost him everything he had, not to mention his life.

Erasmus - Knowledge by Association

Erasmus

Hello Mr. Scott

Thanks for the videos. I enjoy them very much.

My name is Erasmus and I live in Denmark. I had a long-time relationship with a Danish woman. We were married and had children, however, we broke up. After we divorced, I met a Thai woman here in Denmark. She's had a Danish passport for many years and she is the one who introduced me to Thailand. I have gone to Thailand for years on my holidays, for family and fun and to learn the language—the Issan language.

Perhaps I'm skeptical, but I already have a bad feeling about this guy.

I have learned much and now I have my feet in both Denmark and Thailand. I give advice about Thailand to *farang* here.

Why do westerners insist on speaking or writing Thai with me?

The phrase khon tang chart or foreigner, is a more polite and acceptable way of referring to a foreigner in Thailand. Thais use the word farang out of habit more than anything else, but some westerners consider the word derogatory. Considering Erasmus has visited Thailand many times and is involved with a Thai woman, I expected him to know this. See what happens when you have expectations?

I give advice to men here who think Thai women are good for them. Some of them think Thai women are easy. This is not the case, but I am just the adviser and try to help people.

Good work from you, but you forget to tell the story from the Thai side.

Erasmus from Denmark

***

Scott

Hello Erasmus,

Thank you for your kind words, but I feel I must set you straight about a few things.

I've been living here nearly 20 years straight. I am not a tourist like you, I don't go back and forth between the US and Thailand, and I have been with far too many Thai women to count. There is a huge difference between taking part in the dating or pay-for-play scenes and having a Thai girlfriend in Denmark. From what you have told me, your experience is extremely limited. You are giving men advice based on your one relationship with a Thai woman living in Denmark, your trips to Thailand and what you've heard from her and others.

Now, as far as telling things from the Thai side, I usually do not tell stories from the Thai side because first, I am not Thai and second, because it is more important to worry about what you want, need and expect before considering what the woman wants. Call me selfish.

I just made a video about a guy who asked me if I thought she wanted money, love, a marriage, or friendship. What about what he wanted?

Instead of going into the relationship worrying about what the woman wants or needs, it's more important to know what you want and need and to set boundaries based on this. What's important is that the man and woman are both happy.

Allow me to explain…If what she wants is inside the man's boundaries, fine, if not, then there's going to be problems. If a man goes outside of these boundaries to give a woman what he wants, there's a phrase for this—codependent. Or as I like to say, he then becomes a **Captain Save-A-Whore**.

It's one thing to be generous and helpful; it's another to give what you don't want to give or are unable to give.

Also, where I come from, you don't treat a woman like she's easy, period. Women have a way of letting men know they want to sleep with them and the last thing a man needs to do with a woman, whatever nationality, is to treat her like trash or like she's easy. This is more common courtesy than advice, however, there is nothing wrong with a man trying to have sex with a woman as long as he understands the word no.

Regards,
Scott

***

Erasmus

Thanks for reply Scott,

I respect you for having lived in Thailand for many years, what I think you miss is the Thai people live here in Denmark for many years and their thoughts about this subject. Many Danish men here are totally into the business of having a Thai lady, Scott. I just try to help.

To me the cultural gap there is the big issue. You are American and I am from Europe. Both are based on Christian values, even if we are not considered religious and that tradition we have. Thais are different. You think I am a novice about Thailand, but I do not think so. I have many male Thai friends and educated couples who have their own businesses and so forth. It is not just bargirls as you think.

I keep it here and not send you long letter as you talk about

Take care and best wishes

Regards,
Erasmus from Denmark

P.S. My experience is many people here have romantic relationships with Thais. Guess the same as old immigrants from Denmark living in USA still think we here live in a Hans Christian Andersen's old country. I have no intension of finding another Thai woman. I am fine here and have a girlfriend in Germany now, but I have friends in Thailand, both Thai and western people. Now by friend Joe from San Diego selling his medical practice and is moving to Thailand to retire. He says any foreigner moving to a foreign country should always have an escape plan.

You are right about the *farang* thing. In your comment, I hate to be called *farang*. I know the word does not always carry a negative connection to it, but I always say I have a name too.

Erasmus from Denmark

***

Scott

Erasmus,

You do not live here and your knowledge is by association, not by actually living in the country. There is a huge difference between coming here on a holiday and living here. Just because you know Thai people in Denmark doesn't mean you're experienced in the ways of Thai women or know much about Thailand. People change when they immigrate to Western countries—they become westernized.

It really doesn't matter though, for what is most important is that we care about what we want, set boundaries and stick to them. Many men who come here don't do this, whether with Thai bar girls or regular women. They get swept away in a whirlwind lust affair and before they know it, they're contemplating marriage and giving the girl everything they have to prove their love.

Anyhow, thanks again,
Scott

***

Erasmus

Right, I do not live in Thailand, but as I told you I have been there for many times at 20 years now. I have good friends there. But I could not settle there permanently. Yes, sorry, I have a little problem with the beautiful girls when I was younger and I admit this. But now I see what happens when Thais come to Denmark and I can see through almost everything. Many are former bar girls here. I may not know much, but I can think for myself.

From what this guy has written so far, his ability to think for himself is scary.

The well educated Thais I know never think about moving to Western countries; other people think here is welfare available.

Let me tell you a little story. Many years ago we were traveling to Pattaya. This was before the big tourist boom, but eventually there were many Americans and European tourists there. I was then in a relationship with at Thai woman I met here in Denmark. I think it was just random that she was Thai, anyway, we where together many years. We took many family members to meet in Pattaya, many of whom had never been outside Isaan. One day, my girlfriend took her 80-year-old father to a go-go bar and he was living it up again. We could never dream of this in my country. First time for me too, at that time.

This was on my first trip to Thailand, eight days in Pattaya, three weeks in Northeast Isaan, between Khon Kaen and Udonthani.

Erasmus from Denmark

***

Final Thoughts

This man's thoughts are like nails on a chalkboard and to be honest, I'm not really even sure what point he is trying to make aside from telling stories from a Thai standpoint. Can a man learn about Thailand by coming here once a year? Of course, but living in a country and having continual day to day interactions and experiences with Thai people is quite different from those

105

experienced by a tourist.

What strikes me as slightly odd is that based on his one relationship with a Thai woman, Erasmus is giving advice to men. I have always felt a bit strange about giving advice to people, but at least I have twenty-plus years in the country and a treasure chest of experiences.

Fernando - A Good Man...Too Good

Fernando

Hi Scott, I met this lady in Bangkok, but I'm not sure what to do with her. I want to be fair and nice, but the thing is, I am not a very good man and don't want to be a user.

***

Scott

How should I respond to this Fernando? If you don't want her or don't want to be a user, what's the problem? Say goodbye, otherwise, take it day by day and don't lose your senses.

***

Fernando

Hi Scott,

Okay. I wasn't looking for love, but I was very tired and went for a Thai massage. I saw her and she was very nice to me. She came back with me and didn't ask for money. At the end she said she loves me and it was very sad, I had to tell her she can't do that because I cannot love her.

To be in love with anyone, the only way is to be very good friends and all I can do is promise not to be with someone else in Thailand, that's it. I don't know if it's going to work or not, but I know if I do something for

107

someone I don't expect anything or I don't do it.

Fernando isn't making much sense. Like I always say, she was fine before she met you and she'll be fine without you!

***

Scott

Fernando,

Do not believe everything they tell you. Just because she's nice doesn't necessarily mean it is real. Also, while I don't doubt you're a charming guy, she went back with you for money. She may not have asked, but the chances are very high she expected it. She either expected you to know she wanted money or was too shy to ask.

Now...even if she went with you because she liked you or just wanted sex, her telling you she loves you is laughable. I say this because no Thai woman in her right mind, or any other woman for that matter, would meet you in a massage parlor, have sex with you, and then tell you she loves you.

She was after something, believe me. It could have been a long term payment, she could have wanted you to offer to take care of her, but she wanted something. This is why you pay them—so they go away and don't start with this rubbish. If it were me I would have laughed in her face and threw her out.

***

Fernando

Thanks for the info Scott.

I think I can stay safe because there is no room for error. I like going to Thailand and having fun; all I expect is some girl who I can get to know. I'll spend a week or two with her when I'm there so I don't go around and spend my money in bars and clubs. I wouldn't mind if I make that someone a bit happy, but I can't fall in love or support anyone. I just can't put everything at risk and I don't care if she finds someone else. So do you think she will understand it and be a good, normal friend for me?

Anyway, thanks for your time.

Fernando

***

Scott

Why does it matter so much that some girl working in a bar is your good, normal friend? Seriously, what does it matter one way or the other? What are you putting at risk, your marriage? Here's the thing to remember: if they work in a bar, massage parlor, go-go, or soapy, whatever, they are there to take care of you. You pay them and go on your merry way. End of story.

They are not there to become friends with, fall in lust with, or to fall in love with. Pay and go. This is what Thai men do and this is what you must do. Pay and go and your time in Thailand will be simple and free from unnecessary drama.

***

Fernando

Yes Scott, you're right, it doesn't matter and I'm not very serious about it. I don't even know when my next trip will be. If she isn't there, someone else will take care of me.

Thanks man,

Fernando

Final Thoughts

This is a perfect example of a guy with good intentions, but who is totally clueless about how the inner workings of a Thai bar girl. Even after spending a week or two showing a man around Thailand, taking him out to dinner, having breakfast in bed, and having sex day after day, night after night, the vast majority of working girls keep their eyes focused on the prize—the money. Of course, there are exceptions, however, in most cases, even if they are head over heels in love (or their version of love), the money comes first. As long as a man is okay with this sort of relationship and he can afford her, then I see nothing wrong with this. But be honest with yourself and assess the relationship for what it is, not what you want it to be.

Gary - Are You a Sycophant?

Gary

Scott,
What about the lethal roads in Thailand?
How about them? Are there any drunk drivers and accidents in the United States? Are their lethal roads in other countries? Are Thailand's bad drivers enough to keep a tourist or expat from visiting or living in the country?
A guy I know was walking along the footpath. A car flew out and hit a girl on a motorbike. She wasn't wearing a helmet so her brain splattered all over the road and her motorbike went flying and hit my friend. He didn't die, but was taken to hospital busted up pretty bad.

Another friend of mine got knocked off his motorbike. No shit, the guy who knocked him off stopped and then backed up over top of him wanting to kill him. He lived long enough to tell the story, but died in hospital.

In the words of another expat, 'This is one crazy mother f'king country. Life is cheap here.' *An Aussie living in Pattaya.*
Life is cheap everywhere.
My Thai lovely told me about Thais hitting someone on the roadway and then backing over them to make sure they finished the job. In Thailand, it's called short-circuiting a liability recovery. Thais know that it is

always a money deal that can last forever and if you don't settle up, you get the Buriram Crew (hit men). Then you disappear. My wealthy hi-so Thai girlfriend said, "You can always go back to America."

Let's be clear, he flew to Thailand once for two weeks and then never saw her again.

It happens in Thailand. As a pedestrian you are at risk. A friend who is an executive with Kimberly Clark was nailed on a Sukhumvit sidewalk by a nut job motorcycle taxi driving on the sidewalk. Jim endured four hours of plastic surgery. He almost lost an eye. Guess what? No accountability in the land of a thousand smirks.

While he is correct, give me a break. This sort of thing does not happen to hundreds of foreigners on a daily basis nor is it only exclusive to Thailand. To say otherwise is rubbish.

If you are a tourist, without travel insurance, you are looking at a USD $100K medical evacuation. They will treat you in Thailand, but don't expect an orthopedic surgeon or plastic surgeon. They will keep you alive. That is it. And they will confiscate your passport until the medical bill is paid in full.

How expensive is travel insurance? If a tourist is paying $5000 for his family to travel to Thailand or a single man is spending $2500 for his airline ticket and 10 days in the country, surely they can afford to purchase travel insurance. Also, not everyone who comes to Thailand lacks insurance. Are the taxpayers and government responsible for more than stabilizing a patient and preparing them for travel? I think not.

While they will ask for your passport, you are not

obligated to give it to them. It is not his to give; it is the
property of the US government.

Okay Scott: F'ck the cheesy/sophomoric accent and attempt at humor. When are you going to tell the real story about the land of a thousand smirks?

Maybe he's just a dick who thinks everything should be given to him?

You mentioned that you were tired of Thai bullshit and the way foreigners are treated. That Bangkok is starting to 'burn you out.' But where is the beef? Bar girls and bank accounts? Idiocy. Are you a man or a Thai sycophant?

***

Scott

Sorry if my video doesn't meet up to your high expectations, but it is what it is, deal with it. Shall I shit all over Thailand to please you?

As far as whether or not I am a Thai sycophant? Please, don't make me laugh.

For those who are wondering what a sycophant is, it's a brownnoser, a person who kisses the ass of another to gain their approval.

The title of the video is "8 Things I Don't Like About Thailand." Nowhere did I say these were the only things I didn't like and nowhere in the title does it contain the word "YOU."

If I want to bitch and piss and moan as much as you do, I could easily do so.

The truck that passes through the neighborhood 4X a day blaring 'Fresh vegetables, fresh vegetables,' the triple pricing scheme at hospitals, the reluctance to accept criticism, the stink eye I get from some Thais, the poor communication skills. I could go on and on and on. Life is what you make of it. If you want to be miserable and spend all your time bitching and moaning, have at it.

I do understand that Thailand has its share of negatives; I don't believe I am disputing this nor do I think this video makes it seem as if Thailand is paradise.

Speaking of hospitals, what about the girl who was walking down Ramkhamhaeng Road and a piece of an overpass cracked off, fell on her head, and rendered her an invalid for as long as she remains alive? She then got the princely sum of approximately $10,000 to cover her round-the-clock care for as long as she stays alive.

What about what happened to me in my apartment? Through no fault of my own, there was a fire and my pregnant wife, my two-year-old son and I were unable to get out and down to safety. What about how while I was lying on the pavement, some piece of shit who thought I would die stole my Omega Seamaster that I had saved for months to purchase? Thieves are everywhere though. A watch can be replaced. The solution is to buy another—I did.

I could piss away my time whining about my life and life in general, but unless it changes the situation doing so is pointless.

I'm still paying physically for my fall and it's more than ten years later. Every minute of every day, I continue to pay. Does it still irritate me that there were no working fire extinguishers and the fire escapes were welded shut because the owners were scared of people running off without paying? Does it bother me that my pregnant wife and son could have died in this fire because of the owner's stupidity? Definitely, but shall I bitch about this forever? I will certainly remember it, but I refuse to let it ruin whatever time I have left of my life.

What about the guy who has to fire his Thai employee because he's a lazy sack of shit, only to have the guy come back on his motorcycle and crack him on the back of the head?

Do you think this shit doesn't happen elsewhere?

I could find on negative after another if I wanted to do so. Again, it's pointless and a waste of time and energy.

Why would you, a fairly affluent man, travel to Thailand without travel insurance? Most intelligent people know that if any insurance they have won't cover them when abroad, travel insurance probably is a good bet. Aside from the time I let my medical insurance lapse for three months, I've never gone without travel or medical insurance. Even if one has insurance in Thailand or elsewhere, the wrong illness or disease can and will still wipe you out. Shall I add this to the laundry list of Thailand's imperfections? Coming from the US, the wonderful land of HMO's and Obamacare? I don't think so pal.

Call me a simpleton, but I lead a relatively laid back lifestyle. I am rarely bothered by Thais, perhaps because I know how to get along with them, perhaps because I know the rules of the game, perhaps because I'm too self-involved, or perhaps because I don't feel the need for vitriolic criticism or responses. I learn from the past and move on.

Is this a crazy country?

It can be, especially if you want it to be. I lived fast

in the past, and now live slow. I prefer the slower, scenic, more peaceful route.

BTW - you have talked about your 'Thai lovely' so often you're made me blue in the face. Granted, you say she paid for your trip to Thailand, she's fine, and she's got money, blah, blah, blah. In the end, she's still mortal and just a fucking woman. Oh, and let's not forget that she was a woman out for the long term score. That last sentence says it all buddy.

When will I tell the real story about the land of a thousand smirks? I have, I do.

As far as being burnt out, I could be wrong, but I believe what I said was I get burnt out more frequently now. Maybe it has to do with aging. Maybe it's because I'm more active. What does it really matter? Better yet, why the hell does it matter to you?

You strike me as someone who has spent a bit of time in Thailand and who now absolutely abhors the place. Aside from your ability to sleep with your Thai lovely.

I don't know what to tell you. Thailand is love-hate for me, there are positives and negatives, and yin and yang… but I still enjoy my life here.

If you don't like the videos, change the channel Gary. It's quite simple, really.

***

Follow the Road

Good response Scott. I don't understand really why Gary said what he said. You more than anyone I know of who is on YouTube gives a clearer no bullshit report on what is happening in Thailand.

116

***

Scott

One more thing Gary...that wasn't a cheesy, sophomoric attempt at humor, that was just me. That accent came out because of the stupidity of the question, not because I was trying to be humorous. If I'm funny, I'm funny, if I'm not, I'm not. I'm not a comedian and I'm not trying to elicit laughs. Maybe this is actually what makes people laugh. I don't know. I'm just the creator of content. I leave the perspective of the video up to the viewers.

***

Allan

Wow....It is amazing how almost everything you point out here as things about Thailand that you find exasperating are the same as what drives me fucking nuts about South Korea.

***

Scott

Allan - I think it's more an expat thing than a country thing. Love-hate.

***

Allan

True....I half agree that there is certainly an element of that, but I have noticed an interesting pattern in the same specific things that bother people when it comes to living in Asian countries, regardless of the Asian country. Of course, this is just my own observation.

117

Scott Mallon

Jackson - Hard Core Statistical Chances

Jackson

I have a letter (question). Have you or others ever researched out a particular subject that has probably never been asked in one of your letters on the YouTube channel?

The question is: What particular business, food, or otherwise would be the best for a 56-year-old male to start/open up? I am 56-years-old and I want to do more than teach English.

While wanting to do more than teaching English is understandable, starting a business as a foreigner in Thailand is much more difficult than starting one in your home country.

I am living in New York and want to get back to Bangkok as soon as possible. When I say research, I mean hard core statistical chances of succeeding in a particular food, bar, retail, or other industry based on competition, capital (input) and luck.

Please help,
Sincerely,
Jackson (NYC)

P.S. You're the best. I would love to say hello someday.

***

Scott

I have some of the information you are looking for in the member's section of my website. I have a Thailand specific 2016 version of a PDF from the World Bank. It's quite informative and will give you a decent head start. Also, you should check with the Thai Board of Investment. They should be able to help you.

In January of 2016, the BOI reported a 78% decrease in investments. Vietnam has been reporting record increases in foreign investments. You might want to approach your goal from a different perspective.

1. The business opportunities you can legally start are limited. Take a look at the prohibited jobs list on my website or at the Ministry of Labor.

2. As with businesses anywhere, the success rate is and rate of return is low. The success of your business, whatever it may be, will be dependent on your qualifications, start-up capital and a host of other variables. If you're one of these guys who think you're going to put $10-$20K into a business and it's going to provide you with a comfortable lifestyle for the rest of your days, you might want to try doing something like this in Cambodia. Getting a visa is easy, the cost of living is comparable to Thailand and their economy is growing rapidly.

3. Countless foreigners have dreams of opening a bed and breakfast, beachside bungalow, coffee shop, internet cafe/guest house, yada yada yada. Most fail. The market is saturated. In my neighborhood alone there are at least 30 or 40 coffee shops, most of which are scraping by.

4. Since you are a foreigner, you are starting out at a disadvantage. Why? Because you are not Thai and you will never be Thai. A trustworthy Thai partner might help, but finding one is risky and your chances are slim. Again, being a foreigner here puts you act a distinct disadvantage.

5. You have a slight advantage; you are American. This means you can might be able to use the Treaty of Amity and possibly own 100% of your business. However, I know one American who opened a business here in Bangkok under the Treaty of Amity and in his words, it was more expensive to start his business because of this, it took far longer than without the treaty, and the Thais officials he dealt with were apathetic.

Although he still lives in Bangkok, he eventually moved his business to Singapore.

In my opinion, the food business is the way to go because we all gotta eat, but you better know what you're doing before you open a restaurant.

The bar business or go-go business or any type of adult entertainment business that relies strictly on tourists are sink holes and a good way to piss away your money. The only foreigners I know who have been successful with bars or go-go bars are those who have spent hundreds of thousands of dollars. In the case of a popular Phuket go-go bar, the owner has spent several million dollars.

It can be done, but these bars are run by foreigners who can afford to lose a considerable amount of money in the beginning, willing and able to continue pumping money into their establishment, and most importantly, who knew the bar business and how things work in

Thailand. All of those I met with no experience in the bar business or who had minimal knowledge of Thailand lost large sums of money and shut down their businesses within two-three years.

The establishments that succeeded were either run by their wives or trustworthy Thais they had known for many years. In all but one of these bars, the owners were on the premises nearly every minute of every day.

I have two buddies who once owned a place in Nana Plaza. At the time they took over the bar, they had lived in Thailand for approximately ten years. By the time they were done paying the staff, the lease, the police, and the rest of their expenses, they were lucky to break even. In their words, the bar was basically a place to keep them busy and where their friends could come to party. It was incapable of supporting one person, much less two.

Thailand is an export heavy economy and exports are declining, personal debt is rising and there is always the risk of political problems. There are numerous, uncontrollable intangibles. In other words, be financially prepared to lose your ass, at least at in the beginning.

Your question was: "What particular business, food, or otherwise would be the best for a 56-year-old male to start/open up?"

Unfortunately, there is no one size fits all answer to your question. Perhaps you would be better off asking the following questions:

What businesses are specifically viable for you?

Which businesses can foreigners legally operate in Thailand?

What acquired skills do you have that could be used

in your business?

How well do you know Thailand and its' business culture?

How much money do you have to spend and how much can you afford to lose?

Ask yourself these questions and any others you can think of and use The Board of Investment to make an informed decision. Of course, don't invest more than you can afford to lose. Hopefully this will get you headed in there right direction.

Final Thoughts

Like many foreigners with a desire to move to Thailand, Jackson is looking to latch onto any type of job that will make a long term stay possible. This I can understand, after all, when I moved to Thailand, I really had no clue what I would do after depleting my initial funds. Somehow, eventually I found my way. Statistics are hardly the answer though.

Statistics are only a small percentage of what a business is composed of and fails to take into consideration various intangibles; hard work, intelligence or lack of it, local laws and regulations, perseverance, funding or the lack of it, and knowledge of the culture.

If the ability to start a successful business was based solely on statistics, everyone would flock to what is the best and easiest business to start, promote their widget and make money hand over first. The truth is, teaching English is one of the easiest ways to make earns living in Thailand. It lacks the glamour of other jobs, the pay is poor, but as long as a person has a degree, they have the capability of making a living in Thailand. This is why a large percentage of expats in Thailand teach English.

Jackson can move to Thailand and teach English to cover his overhead while studying statistics at his leisure. When his knowledge of Thailand and its' business practices are solid, then maybe, just maybe, he can start a business involving something he likes and is good at and turn it into a prosperous enterprise.

Jay - Once Is Enough

Jay

Hi Scott,

Fantastic photos of your travels in Thailand and Asia. I've been watching your YouTube videos; they're funny and most of all interesting and helpful. Well, it's my twelfth trip to Thailand up to now and in that time, I've learned a lot about Thailand and the culture. Okay, when I first came to Thailand I did not understand why all these beautiful ladies in the night clubs and bars just fell in love so quickly.

I hold my hand up, yes, I married a bar girl and we divorced after six months. Yes, I sent money too, to take care of her, a few hundred pounds every month. It worked out to about 10,000 baht, which is more than your average 7/11 wage. Lucky for me she was knockin' the old man off with more money upstairs. Lucky I found this out and we agreed to finish and take care of the marriage papers down at the local offices. Oooossshhh.

That was a close one. But it's ok, I was learning.

The Golden Rule - Do not get emotionally involved with a prostitute. Had he followed this tenet, he would have saved you quite a bit of aggravation. Alas, many-a-man has tried to buck the system and turn a whore into a housewife. Inevitably the majority end in failure.

As time went by I learned the language bit by bit.

Still learning now, lol, and I got the bar scene out of my system. Well, at least the bar girls. I still enjoy a visit too Sin City (Pattaya) once in a while. In one sense it has everything, the beach, night life, food and less rainfall.

Most of all, I love jumping in with my girlfriend and seeing proper Thailand, Thai style. And yes, you're right Scott. A Thai lady with a good job, not a bar girl or girl working in a massage parlor. A girl who loves you for your heart and who never asks for money every month. Yes, there is such lady in Thailand. I am very happy I learned the hard way because I found a good Thai lady who respects me and I respect her.

Keep the good work up Scott, love the videos.

****

Scott

Jay - thanks for watching and for writing. At least you came out somewhat unscathed. I'm sure it could have been much worse. One thing though...if you have a good Thai woman, no matter what she says about it being okay to go with the occasional hooker, do not throw it in her face. Be discreet. She might say doing so is okay, but chances are, it's not.

As one grows older, running around with women becomes a much lower priority. There are too many other important things to spend your time doing. Anyway, this is what massage parlors are for...get a massage, get your needs taken care of, and out the door you go, without the hassles of a mistress or second girlfriend or whatever. Far less complicated.

Scott

***

Jay

Hi Scott,

Thanks for the reply. About the massage, the extras don't interest me. I just like a good Thai style massage. People get the wrong idea about when you say you are going to Thailand.

"Oh really, what are you going there for?"

Okay, at first, I was like a dog in heat, but after a few years, all the lies the working girls tell you get boring. When you know all the tricks in the book, you treat them as such or as they treat you. Like you said, go in, get what you desire, feed them a load of bull shit and get out of there ASAP. When you know the truth, life is a lot easier.

You need to have more than knowledge of the truth, you need to believe it and be willing to deal with it appropriately. The men who have problems can usually acknowledge the red flags and yet instead of drawing a line in the sand and moving on, they linger in the relationship and accept whatever happens.

Dealing with them is even more amusing when you understand what they are up to. Having said all that, I never look down on them because we are all equal and I understand the bar girls have to take care of their families. But if you know what it's all about, it is good fun.

Scott, I have been thinking about different ways of making a living in Thailand. What do you suggest?

Jay

***

Scott

This is the million dollar question and it all depends upon your skills and marketability. Jobs are limited. You really need to find your own way or you'll end up as an old ass English teacher, usually making peanuts.

***

Jay

Lol, yes it is probably best to make my money in England. I don't fancy being stuck in a hot classroom for 20,000 baht a month. Thanks for the reply. Take care.

Final Thoughts

As I stated earlier, Jay was very lucky to come out of the relationship unscathed. It could have been much worse. She could have driven him to take a header off the third floor of Nana Plaza; left him broke and made his life miserable for years. Fortunately, he seemed to have learned his lesson and he will be more careful in his future relationships.

Jimmy - Should I Be Alarmed?

Jimmy

Dear Scott,
I would appreciate it if you can give me any help.
I have another Thai love story…It doesn't get old *na*?
Actually, it's been old for quite some time. For fifty-plus years men have been coming to Thailand and indulging in the feminine fruit, and for fifty years men have been telling of their heartbreaks and love affairs!

By the way I really enjoy your videos and have been watching for quiet sometime. My name is Jim, I am 22 years old and I am Thai/Australian. In about nine days time I am about fly to Thailand to meet a girl I met online from thailovelinks.com We plan to spend two days in Bangkok, then travel to her home in Udonthani and stay for a month. She is a university graduate, can speak, write and read English and has a good head about her. Plus, she is quite attractive, 23 years old and comes from a well-to-do Thai family. I have been getting to know her by means of telephone, line chat and video call. We agreed to be in a relationship on Facebook since last October and we literally act and behave as if I am already her boyfriend.

Isn't that special?

I am aware she does have legitimate male friends that she converses with and she has conversations with other men on Facebook. Some of what I have read on

Facebook suggests they are more than friends. She is constantly bombarded with compliments and arse-kissing from typical, young, horny Thai boys. Occasionally, a sex crazed foreigner will speak to her, making all sorts of demanding requests. I think you have general idea. Anyway, being ex-army, I am patient and letting her interactions unfold so I know more about her true self.

Anyway, my question is, more than once I have caught her online speaking to other single men, both Thai and foreigner. What alarms me is her willingness to give into their requests (i.e., send photos, exchange numbers, communicating on social internet apps, etc.) fairly easily. I believe she thrives on the attention from multiple men and she is even inclined to flirt back. She has no hesitation, but as far as I can tell, she has not followed through on anything. To my horror she told other men she was still single even after agreeing to be in an online relationship with me, but she has stopped talking to all of them in the past two weeks. From what my recon has shown, although she is flirty, she has no other serious man in her life except me. Only yesterday I read a message on her Facebook chat she mention to a Thai guy that he was "cute" and sent him a love heart image and he did replied with additional arse kissing images. This is not the only example at least a Half dozen other men have talked to her like this since I have been getting to know her. I know I may be playing the jealous, angry boyfriend perhaps and I know we are not entirely serious yet because we have yet to meet physically.

But should I be alarmed about this girl I am spending

time with for a month? Or is it normal for Thai girls to be flirty by nature? I don't believe this behavior is of the norm for a woman who says they are in a relationship with me or from my previous experience with Thai women.

You answered your own question; you just don't want to see the writing on the wall. You are allowing her to start off this quasi-relationship how she wants while you are left scratching your ass. If you have to write someone else (me) to ask if the relationship is normal, do you think her actions are acceptable. I wouldn't put up with this and if she truly cares about you, she would stop immediately.

My gut instinct says she will continue this behavior because she can't help herself, this girl is gorgeous she knows she is beautiful and loves attention. Although I can't control her actions, I have mention to her this is the last straw. I have threatened to cease all talk and cancel my trip to meet her. I may be a young guy but I feel my intentions for a pure relationship are sincere and I don't deserve a girl who makes it easy for other men to exploit her. That's just the way I am.

I am concerned, but maybe I am over reacting. Any reply will be appreciated

Cheers mate

Chok dee lae jer gan mai (Good luck and until next time)

Jimmy

***

Scott

Hello Jimmy,

131

I don't think you're overreacting. Flirting is one thing. Involving herself with other men is another matter, especially when you are both supposed to be in a relationship. Don't come to Thailand just to see her. Also, there is no need to go to Udonthani for your entire stay. I've lived there and know the area pretty well. It is a poor regions and many of the women there are looking to do a George Jefferson and move it on up. If you're coming to Thailand, regardless of what happens with her, great. Just see how it plays out and YOU call the shots. If she doesn't like it, gorgeous or not, you need to tell her to take a hike.

Good Thai women aren't going around sending little hearts to men they don't know unless they are attention whores or are looking for men to sponsor them.

Good luck,
Scott

***

Jimmy

Hi Scott,
Thanks for your reply. I consider myself mature and open minded enough to find any women I want in Thailand. I have had brief relationships with women before although quite older than me. I don't believe it will be hard for me to find somebody else if things go sour.

Thanks again,
Jimmy

***

Jimmy

Hey Scott,

I have just finished watching your video about myself and your advice about my situation. I must say I found some of the other YouTuber comments about me slightly amusing! But you know I am open to criticism, every relationship is different and mine is far from perfect. Perhaps people should review their own lives and relationship before they sound like the love gurus behind their computer desk giving me advice—just saying! I laughed my ass off at the wanker who commented that I am head over heels for her. Ha, ha, and for everybody's information my Thai mother (who is also an excellent women) has taught me many things about Thai women and life, but I am still teaching myself more. I want to be clear again, I am young guy, I know this, but I feel the relationship I desire is beyond my age of 22 years. I am mature, I feel, and I am quite established in my life and my career. My experience has taught be to wary, open minded and to be self-motivated. How many of your viewers can say they have to sign a will at the age of 18? I honestly feel the only part missing in my life is love and I am willing to explore and find the right women to share my life with.

Anyway, I am here now in Udon and have already spent a week with her and her family. Life in Udon is exactly what I have pictured it to be, pretty much the same as my past experience living in Uttaradit. She has accepted what she has done wrong, and since meeting her she has shown me she wants to commit to a relationship (behaving sensibly online and in person). She has been upfront and open with me on the subject about love/relationship and what we hope maybe for the future. I mentioned before she has a good head about her, she doesn't want to commit to anything beyond girlfriend-boyfriend relationship as yet because we are still exploring our compatibility.

Although we are mature enough to joke about *sin sod*, conversation with her family has been pretty much the same. She is not money motivated, like her family. Her family just wants for her to be happy with a man that will treat her respectably and genuinely loves her. Even though we have had a few hiccups in our relationship I feel we are compatible and a good relationship will not be difficult because we understand each other well. I am not madly in love or signing my life away as some of viewers may think! I think it is appropriate for me to share this—her younger sister who is 20 is about to meet a Taiwanese guy next week from ThaiLoveLinks. This guy speaks zero English—the same with her sister—and already he wants to pay 10 million baht for *sin sod*. Yes, ten big ones, holy fuck! So you see there are other guys worst off than me! Ha-ha, but that's their relationship so what happens between them doesn't concern me or my own relationship.

Anyway, I am happy here, I am falling in love but I am still open-minded to everything. I just thought I would send this message to let you know how my situation is going. I appreciate your time Scott.

Thanks,
Jimmy

***

UPDATE

Scott

Hey Jimmy,

Just wondering - what ever happened with your girl in Udonthani?

Scott

***

Jimmy

Hi Scott,

We are both living Australia now. After a long wait, her visa was approved and she has been here

since Nov 2015. All that other drama has surpassed. Every relationship is different and I am glad we were able to turn over a new leaf. Once I met her and got to meet her family we actually gelled and grew into a 'normal couple'. We laugh, we play, we work together and we fight, I believe nothing is out of the norm from any other relationship.

Hope things are well on your end my friend; I have tuned out of your videos after your Burma visit but every now and then drop back into your channel for an update. Maybe next time I am in Bangkok I will come and visit you and your wife.

Also, I have been extremely busy the past eight months with a career change. I now work in the immigration division here—lots of people to detain and lots of people to be removed!

Hope this message finds you well.

Regards my friend,
Jimmy

***

Scott

Hey Jimmy,

Wow, that's fantastic. Congratulations.

My wife and I went to Bali in March, and then in April/May we went with our two sons to the US - Florida and New York. This was their first time to the US so it was quite an experience. I'm sure your girl is settled in by now. It doesn't take long.

Anyhow, glad to hear things are going well and you are still together.

All the best,
Scott

Final Thoughts

I have never been a fan of online dating. Long-distance relationships are a pain and when it comes to relationships with women from Thailand and other poor countries in the world, there are too many schemers and scammers and I never liked wasting my time. Better to date the old-fashioned way: meet in person, get the woman's phone number, have a few conversations, go out, and see where it goes.

Online dating and long-distance relationships work for some people. I think this one may have worked because they are both Thai. When a man lives in the US, getting to know a woman living in a foreign culture can be trying. It takes two strong, willing, trusting people who know what they want to make an online relationship work.

Western-Thai online relationships usually fail before they get started. As this letter illustrates though, there are occasionally happy endings.

Kris - I'm a Little Worried

Kris

Hi Scott!

I have seen some of your videos on YouTube. After falling in love with a girl in Thailand, I would like to ask you a little about it since you seem to have some knowledge about this, and hopefully the time for it too. I'll try to make it short and be brief.

He tried and failed, big time.

I was in Phuket a few weeks ago where I met a girl in a massage shop located in Bangla Road. I was with her for eleven days and she is already talking about our future, marriage and kids, etc. in a few years, though. She is not so pushy about this and as I told her, I want to take it slowly.

She says she has two kids, but they stay with her family and they take care of them. I think she is sending her family some money every month for this.

These are the type of things he needs to know before ever thinking about getting involved in a serious relationship with her!

She is talking about coming to Norway to stay with me, beginning with getting a tourist visa or whatever it is called. I am about to start at a part-time job that will become a full-time job after several months. I am not sure what kind of documents I will need to provide the immigration office to make this happen, so she can come here (at least a few months to start with), but I am worried I will have to document that I have a lot of cash to be able to support her while she stays here. I wanted to ask you about this. Do you have any idea? I know Norway is probably not quite the same as USA when it comes to this, but maybe it is a bit similar?

The answer to this question should come later, after he actually knows her and knows the answers to some other questions he asks me.

The thing that worries me the most is that she is asking me for support.

After only eleven days, she is asking for support. Granted, some Thai women will actually ask for support the first night, but still, he is blind as a bat. The signs are already showing, and yet he is so immersed in this pseudo-relationship he is completely adrift. This poor, sad fellow needs to learn a little about women before getting into a relationship.

First, she would like 20,000 baht per month for six months to learn English. She will also go home, which is in Northern Thailand, to stay with her family while she waits for the visa. She will not be working at this time, but still I think this is too much to pay. What do you think?

Now here is what I don't get. He thinks this is too much to pay, and instead of having the gonads to tell her she's out of her mind, he writes me (of all people) seeking validation of what he believes.

I don't know how much English classes cost.

So find out! Go online, check around!

She plans on living with her parents while not working, but it still seems like a lot of money to me.

Maybe this is just so she can buy what she wants, but maybe she can manage with less. Maybe 15K baht per month or even 10K baht. I am just so worried, because in the long run it is still going to be a lot of money for me, and I am living by myself.

What does this tell you? Grow a sack and tell her it's been nice knowing her, you had a wonderful eleven days, and maybe you'll see her again one day. You are but two ships passing in the night! Perhaps he should have read Longfellow.

"Ships that pass in the night, and speak each other in passing, Only a signal shown and a distant voice in the darkness; So on the ocean of life, we pass and speak one another, Only a look and a voice, then darkness again and a silence."

Tales of a Wayside Inn (1863)
Henry Wadsworth Longfellow,
***

She also mentioned at one point paying around 200,000 baht to buy her from her family. This seems strange to me. I know Thailand and Europe are not the same culture, but still.

Bottom line I guess, is do you know something I can ask her to try find out if she is just another gold digger or if she is for real? I want to make sure she really wants to try and make a future with me.

If he is this worried, why would he even consider giving her anything?

I would say I am pretty good at sensing if a person is trying to scam me or not, although I know, I know, love can blind a person very easily. She just seems so real about it all and seems to really love me too.

I am worried because she is first trying to get 120,000 baht or so from me in support even before she goes to Norway. Then later on she wants a baby with me for my genetics and then after we get married, she will ask for a divorce because she will gain money or something.

I just wished there were some things I could ask her to try and find out if she is for real or not. I don't know if you just find what I am writing to be stupid or will ignore it or whatever, but I would really appreciate a comment or anything. What do you think? Is she is for real? Does she just need me to support her so she can actually learn English and then to go to Norway? Does she really want to make it all happen for a good future with me? Are her intentions good? Is there anything I can ask or talk with her about to find out about this? Or is it like, "It's not worth the risk mate, just forget about her?" She could be my future wife, but it is a really big risk to take. Please help me with some input on this. A comment or anything would be appreciated a lot!

Thanks for your time!

Best regards,
Kris

***

Scott

Hi,

Wow…you're in a spot and it's a spot you do not need to be in. First, what is it you want from her? Second, she works in a massage parlor. This is not good.

She's known you eleven days. Don't you think that no matter whom you're with or where you're with them, eleven days is way, way too fast to start thinking of marriage? She's after a provider; she's not necessarily after you. Plain and simple, she is after someone who will take care of her, anyone.

After only a short period of time she is asking for a monthly stipend and talking about sin sod. Again, this is not good. She has been married and has kids. She shouldn't be asking for any sin sod, at all. A Thai man wouldn't pay it and neither should you. The only way you should ever pay this is if you've known her for a long period of time and if the family promised to give all or most of it back.

She's talking of coming to Norway. In three words— don't do it. She's setting the hook right now. If she gets you to bring her there, it's more time for her to talk you into marriage and honestly, I would not put myself out for her. If she wants to go to Norway, tell her to pay for the ticket and she can stay with you for a week or two. Of course, this isn't going to happen. If you do bring her over, my guess is you're going to have to provide some sort of bond so that if she runs off or causes any problems, the government can get the money from you. Each country is different and while I do know a Swede from many years ago who used to bring girls to Sweden to see him, he was in no way thinking of marrying them. He brought them for fun, they knew this, and he never talked of marrying a girl from a massage parlor.

As far as the 20K baht per month, this is quite a bit, especially since you barely know her. Listen, a decent Thai woman would never ask for money right off the bat or ask you to take care of them like this unless you had been together for quite some time and were in a serious relationship.

Asking for support immediately upon meeting a person his is what whores do. I'm sorry to say this but it's the truth. Most Thai women do not say, "Give me this much money every month and we can be together." They may ask or hint at some sort of support once you've known them for while, but asking within a few days of meeting is not really proper in Thai culture.

Anyway you look at it, this is a mistake. Tell her no to the monthly assistance, tell her no to marriage and tell her that you want to be friends for a year or two and then maybe you'll think about it. If she sticks around, then maybe she's worthwhile. If she leaves or gets mad, you know what she's after.

You are the man. You call the shots, not her. Do not let her dictate any of the terms, period.

All the best,
Scott

***

Kris

Hi Scott!

Thanks for the reply.

What I am looking for in this girl is primarily a girlfriend or wife, but I am so in love with her that I would actually be happy even if she could just come visit me in Norway for a few months. I just want to be with her and have some fun with her, and then in the future, maybe after a year or two years, I will consider marriage with her. Of course, only if I feel comfortable with the relationship and by then, trust her enough.

To be honest with you, she works in a massage parlor

in a place that caters to men on Bangla Road, and after being in Thailand a little while and looking beyond the being blinded by love, I realize how crazy this is.

I was a little drunk when I first met her there, agreeing to a massage, and not long after, she offered me anything I wanted for 3000 baht. Thinking back on it, I feel very sure that in the past she has done similar things with other men. So I am sure she offered massages and happy endings. She goes to check for HIV and everything else every three months just to be 100%, certain she is clean, and I guess there is a reason for this. She has probably been doing happy endings, mainly for the money to be able to support her with food and what not. Seems like some days, at least in the low season, she makes very little money. Some days, she tells me she had no customers. "Not good," she says.

I talk with her on video chat on the phone for many hours every day, and it is hard to focus on other things, like work and other important things. She has me wrapped up pretty good, even now, although I have known her for only this little time. Having declared our relationship and what not on Facebook, and even meeting my family on video chat, it all seems good. She actually is interested in me for who I am. I am trying not to be scammed, but it feels like I either go the whole way or its full stop.

At one point I sent her a text message on her phone asking about the two kids she has and asked if they are both from the same man or two different guys. She was quick to get ill-tempered and then would not answer my calls. She sent me messages like "I no good for you," and "Thanks for you, goodbye," etc., and when she finally picked up the phone, she was crying, I managed to calm her down and get her to realize that this was a misunderstanding because of her poor English. I told her that I just wanted to know, not that I was being negative or unsure of her and it was soon all good again.

Wait a second! He is unsure of her! Isn't this the very reason why he emailed me? This man is so whipped that even though he knows she is not good for him and he doesn't trust her, he still can't say no.

What worried me at this point was things like, what if I do go the whole way with support and all, and after having sent her a lot of money in the long run, she turns so fast with this temper of hers and says, 'Thanks for you, goodbye.'

I am even more worried about trusting her like this. Of course, maybe this is different and in the long run after knowing her a little longer she will not change her mind so easily, but I don't think she is worth the risk. The only reason why I am unsure is because I am so in love with her and don't want to lose her. One side of me is saying this is crazy, she is probably a whore with two kids and has been married before. Like, what am I doing? What is wrong with me? I have never met such a killer girl and I have had the best time of my life with her when I was with her in Thailand, but I guess I can find a much better woman, without kids and who hasn't been married before. But I don't know this and to be honest, the thought of not hearing her voice again kills me inside. Maybe she just has me hooked too darn well.

Ya think? Men like this need a hard slap—they really need to use their brains instead of their emotions. Wake up Chowderhead!

She is talking about marriage in the future, but yeah it's still very far out there to even bringing it up so early feels strange. The same goes with having a kid with her in the future and *sin sod*. She was talking about this after like a week or so after we met!

Another thing is that one time I paid 20K baht to her for a booking, as she called it. I guess this was because she was with me all day, every day and was not at work making the business money. Then when I left for home, I actually gave her another 16K baht. So a total of 36K baht directly to her, plus I paid for everything when she was with me, Food, clothes, the hotel, etc., so yeah, I guess for her this is a lot of cash and maybe she sees me as a walking ATM, or something like it. She kept saying, "You're a handsome man," all the time, so I guess maybe she is thinking to herself that I am an okay looking guy with a lot of money, let's see how much money I can get out of him, or something like this, I don't know.

Soon she will call me again and I am going to tell her that it's all going too fast for me. I have said before that I am okay to give her support, but this was because I was too blinded by love at that point. I am going to tell her that I am willing to pay for her flight ticket back and forth to Norway, and of course, take care of everything while she is here. This way we can get to know each other better, before getting so serious. I am not okay sending her 20K baht every month for six months before comes to Norway.

He is not okay with sending her the 20K a month, but he just cannot let go!

If she gets mad or something, then yeah, I understand

that it was mainly all about the money. If she gets sad, and says it is okay to take it slower, I still won't know if she is after the money, but at least then there won't be so much pressure for money from me anymore. Then maybe, I can get to know her much more and spend more time with her without having to pay this crazy amount of money first for a relationship to happen and we can just take it from there.

Am I the only one who views his logic as extremely screwed up? The woman took more than $1000 USD from him, 3000 baht to have sex with her, she wants 20K baht a month and although he doesn't trust her and he feels they're moving too fast, he's still going to fly her to Norway. He has known her for eleven days. Maybe, just maybe he lives in some frozen wasteland with no women and he is willing to do anything for a woman by his side. Hard to imagine, but this scenario would make his line of thinking slightly more plausible.

She told me her parents are poor farmers living in Ubon and she isn't making much money either. So she could be for real, but yeah, it's not likely. I still don't know for sure. This is why I am willing to pay for her ticket to Norway and to pay for her expenses while she is here.

I think you are right though. This is probably a big mistake, but I am willing to give her a chance now that this silly amount of money she wants to be paid beforehand is out of the picture. Thinking to myself that I am such a lowlife seeking love from a poor whore from Thailand like this, I guess it is the love thing that is driving me.

Lust and the inability to have her when he wants are driving him mad. He is worried if he doesn't take this poor maiden out of the bar scene, he might lose her forever. Would that really be such a bad thing? All I can do is wish them good luck.

Thanks a lot for your input, it opened my eyes a little and confirmed the fact that the monthly support is just crazy and therefore a no-go. It also confirms to me that it is still very crazy to proceed with this relationship, but I think if I go slowly and carefully and I give her the chance, I can see if it turns out to be all about the money for her. Then it is not as much of a loss as it would have been otherwise.

In your eyes, is there really no chance that this girl could be for real? I mean, she is poor, living under conditions where her life is never good life for her, so maybe there is a chance that she actually likes me and wants to try and make a future with me? To have a better life for herself?

Notice he never once mentions her children having a better life or his raising them.

She and I have done so much together in the little time I was in Thailand, everything from going to Phi Phi Islands to driving around through cities on motorbikes, doing just about anything and having a great time. I am sure she had a really good time too and this was real. Man, it is almost too hard for me to let her go and I am just looking for a way to give her a chance without taking major risk. It is just so hard for me! This is why your input is appreciated so very much.

I don't have anyone else to talk about this with because I realize she probably used to sell sex sometimes for money and it's just too fucked up to talk about it with friends or family.

What does this say? And notice how he says, 'She probably used to sell sex sometimes for money.' He just cannot bring himself to look at what is almost certainly the truth. In fact, what he is trying to do is make their eleven days into more than the brief fling that it was.

"I am sure she had a really good time too and this was real"

¡Ay Chihuahua! You can lead a horse to water, but you can't make him drink. This guy wants to hear my advice; he just doesn't want to act on it.

She tells me that she is only giving massages and nothing else; as she knows I don't like the idea of her even massaging other men. I can never trust her 100%, but I believe she is keeping her word, honestly I thinks she really is. She seems for real, but I just cannot know for sure, and she has agreed to change her profession later, as I don't like her giving massages for money.

She seems really fond of the idea of living and working in Norway as in her view it is a good place for making money. I just wished there was a way for me to find out if her intentions are good or if she is just a gold digger. I will try to proceed with her as carefully as I can while still giving her a chance.

She turned 30 years old yesterday. I am 27 myself, and the fact that she is actually my first girlfriend is sad enough in itself, but I guess this is why I'm being so blinded by love and why I am so scared of losing her.

I am sorry for the long mail with so many details. I just don't have anyone to talk with about this. Thanks <u>a lot</u> again! Your input makes me open my eyes a little more and to remember to be more careful. Also, I do get how crazy and stupid this is, but maybe this is what will save me in the end, that I think about what I have been told. Maybe in the last minute before taking any big risk I will come to my senses and call it all off. I don't know.

Best regards,

***

Scott

Why would you love a woman who:

1. Probably doesn't even know what real love is.

2. Is after ANY man who will support her.

3. Has been with so many men you can't bring yourself to talk about her with other people, including your family?

4. Who is probably going to cause you heartache?

5. Is emotionally unstable and extremely immature.

What you are feeling is not love.

Do not be fooled by her crying and her lack of responses to your valid questions.

Her being poor does not mean you should take care of her. Taking care of a prostitute who either acts or actually is in desperate need of help is what is known as the Captain Save-a-Ho syndrome.

She was fine before you met her and she'll be fine when you're gone, believe me. My guess is you will not listen to my advice no matter what I say.

All I can say is good luck.

Scott

You really, really, really NEED TO WAKE UP!

***

Kris

Hi! Thanks again for the reply.

150

Yes, I know you are right. It is just plain stupid of me and she is not actually worthy of me. I realize this now. It is all just a big waste of time and money.

I didn't get the chance to talk seriously with her last night because she had a headache and went to sleep early, but I am going to have a chat with her after she is finished with work tonight.

Knowing that she is most likely only after the money/support and is a whore, I would still like to try and have her over once for 2-3 months to have some good time and fun with her before I tell her this isn't going to work. I will do this without sending her any money or anything beforehand, only paying for the flight ticket and for her to stay here.

Thinking about it though makes me want to ask you if you know about any red flags or something to look out for while she is here. I was thinking that if she agrees to come over for a few months to get to know each other a bit better first, and I haven't given her any support like she wanted to, that maybe she will try to ask me for some expensive stuff while here to sell later on or keep or whatever. Do you know someone that has done similar things and where it went wrong in a way while she was in his country? It's the first time for me having a woman coming to my country like this, and I am thinking that maybe there are some things I should be thinking of or looking out for while she is here. I would appreciate it very much if you have any knowledge about this!

I will be working while she is here and gone for like seven hours every day, while she is alone in the apartment, this worries me a bit. Although I don't think she will do something stupid, I cannot know this for sure. Wondering if there are any precautions I can take to try and lower the chances for this, other than not bringing her over at all.

I don't mind if you make a video of this, glad if my stupid story can be of any help for others, and I can't tell you how much I appreciate you even taking your time for this, because for me, it might be what actually saves me from doing a huge and horrible mistake.

If he believes it might be a huge and a horrible mistake, what does this say?

I just want to be with her at least a few months more before ending it, without having to give her any huge amount of money, or take any major risk or something, but I'm guessing these are not options, because just bringing her over here and leaving her alone in the apartment for like seven hours every day is big enough risk as it is.

If I bring her over for say, three months, what you think is the worst thing that can happen? Although I can never be 100% certain, I am pretty sure about her not running off, doing something stupid while I am not here or such.

Thank you again for your time Scott!

Best regards,
Kris

***

Scott

If it's so stupid and such a waste of time, not to mention she's not worthy of you, why in the world would you bring her back to Norway? You're so in love with her, right? She will use that time in Norway with you to change your feelings and make you see things her way, believe me. You know it and I know it. If you bring her over for three months, you're pissing away time on a girl in a relationship that isn't going anywhere, or at least shouldn't. Not only this, you can't even trust her!

Have some self-esteem man. Seriously, she's a whore, she is out for your money, you know it's not a good situation, and yet you still feel the need to bring her to Norway. You do not need her, period. Again wake up Chowderhead! Grow some balls!

The red flags are all there, you just refuse to see or believe them. You don't even know if you can trust her in your apartment and you're still thinking of letting her stay with you for no other reason than you want to be with a woman.

Like I told you, grow some balls, understand there will be other women, and stop obsessing and letting this whore lead you around like a puppy dog. I don't know any other way to put it.

Good Luck,
Scott

Final Thoughts

This letter really got me thinking. The object of the sender's affection requested three thousand baht from him for sex, she works as a masseuse in a tourist area where a revolving door of tourists come from around the world to drink and screw whores. The only other places in Thailand that match Phuket's prostitution scene are Pattaya and Bangkok. Sure, there are many, many hardworking women with more mainstream jobs working in Phuket, but most tourists lack the time and language skills necessary to meet and get to know any of them.

This woman was working in a massage parlor and he paid her for sex during their first encounter. How special is this man to her? I could be wrong—I don't think I am though—but he is simply a turn, a number, and a possibility of a better life. Hard to fault a woman making a living as a masseuse who gives happy endings, but this is all he is, a way out. She could grow to love him, who knows, but she is a woman struggling in life and struggling to take care of her children and this is far from her first rodeo. Nothing wrong with what she was doing, however as is the case with many men who visit or live in Thailand, he did his thinking with the little head as opposed to the big one.

When a man accepts a woman who is actively working as a prostitute to be his future wife and the mother of his children, what does this say about him?

This guy has known the woman for less than two weeks and he's already considering sponsoring and marrying her! He admits his unwillingness to trust her in his home, he admits knowing she is probably a whore, and yet he is still willing to fly her halfway around the world so he has a woman, even if it is only temporary.

Men like this are so desperate they are willing to do almost anything just to be with a woman. They are the sucker born every minute, or as I like to say, men without a sack.

At best, this woman was struggling to feed her family and felt she had no other options. Rarely is this true of women selling their bodies in the tourist areas geared towards the foreign market. Before you call me cold-hearted, take a look at the average bar girl, or whore, if you prefer. Does she own an expensive phone and is she slathered in gold? Does she blow her money partying with her friends or gambling? How much is she really sending to her family to take care of her children or her own parents? Once you find out the answers to these questions, if possible, you can then determine whether or she choose to work in the sex industry to survive, family pressures, or because she is lazy and unwilling to do what many other women around the country do, work in an office or factory or selling clothes at a local market.

There are many reasons women work as bar girls. Does this mean a man should feel sorry for them and accept responsibility for them? Feeling compassion for another human being's situation is understandable. Countless foreigners have offered opportunities to a bar girls to better their lives through school or employment, only to have them fritter away the chance.

Looking for a girlfriend and future wife should not feel the same as taking care of a child. If I wanted a child instead of a wife, I would get a dog.

Everywhere in the world, the shortage of money is a focal point of life. This woman tried to persuade him into a quick marriage, for a fee of course, and from the way he has described it, the entire relationship was about money, money, money! She is a whore, this is indisputable, and in my humble opinion, she saw an opportunity to take advantage of an overly needy man too weak to say no. The sender of these letters is an excellent example of a weak man unwilling to believe what was in front of his own two eyes.

Kris - She Calls Me Babe or Baby

Kris

Hey Scott,
Sawadee krap.

I have been watching many of your videos on YouTube recently and I am impressed with your knowledge and tell-it-like-it-is attitude. Of course, I watch your videos because I am interested in going to Thailand soon and possibly becoming an English teacher there with a degree in teaching English. From the research I have done it sounds like Thailand is a great place for the opportunity and lifestyle that I want to have. I'm hoping to also run a few businesses on the side like maybe owning a condo block and renting it out to tourists or locals. These are just ideas that I have so far.

A little about myself, I am 21 years old soon to be 22 in May, but I have a strong desire to learn and experience different cultures and lifestyles. I am a survivor of Hodgkin's disease, so I have started transitioning to an all Vegan diet and I now refrain from tobacco and other drugs. I'll be honest with you; I do find Asian women to be very attractive. I have dated quite a lot of women here in the states, (mostly Latinas) and I am very sexually experienced for my age. I have gotten the animalistic urge to have sex with every girl I see out of my system by now and I would like to settle down with someone special, but I have yet to find a girl here in the states who I feel like I could stay with.

What's wrong with this guy? He's only twenty-one and the animalistic urge is gone already?

From having watched a lot of your videos, I know you tell people to stay away from bar girls and girls whom hang out a lot in bars or that work in bars. I have started talking to a very cute Thai girl that works in a cafe that serves alcohol. I don't know if it's a bar specifically, I think she said it was a cafe. I am friends with her on Facebook and we talk over a messenger app on my phone most of the time. We have talked on Skype a couple of times before, but most of the time she is at a bar when we talk. From her pictures on Facebook, it looks like she likes to spend a lot of times at bars. I met this girl on a pen pal website and we have been talking for almost a year.

So he hasn't even met her. I can smell what's coming next.

What confuses me though, is she likes to call me babe or baby, and when I send her pictures, she says I am lovely and cute. We have exchanged many photos of each other. From our conversations I have come to the conclusion that her English is not very good, but she wants me to teach her English for now. I have seen pictures of her with her family on Facebook and through talking to her it looks like she comes from a very hard working and loving family.

How would he really know?

I want to teach English in Thailand and own a farm and I have told her this. She says her family grows a lot of their own food and this speaks to me, because I feel like she has a good heart from what she has said.

However, she has also said that she wants to own a bar for her career.

Why not just cut to the chase and get married? I'm joking. He hasn't even met this girl and he's already determined she has a good heart. He's a Chowderhead.

You say stay away from bar girls but are there exceptions to certain types of bar girls?

I have talked to her about coming to the United States. She is interested and she has told me a couple of times that she is not afraid to work. I can't tell if she is being honest or just lying to me. I have never met this girl in person nor have I been to Thailand yet. I just wanted to get your take on this girl and help me figure out if I should keep talking to her, because maybe she is one of those good-girl wife material types of girls.

Imagine me banging my head on the wall right now, because this is exactly what I am doing.

I have also told her that I want to learn Thai and she has said that she was bored of speaking her native language, hence her desire to learn English. She has shown signs that she is interested in me other than what I have stated in this e-mail. I know this girl is not a prostitute or a lady boy for a fact. I wanted some insight on this girl. So far she has only met one of the signs that you said I should stay away from. So if you can tell me if this girl is a keeper or just another bar girl I would be very thankful. I hope you email me back, I am a big fan of your videos, and they have helped me out a lot.

Have a nice day and keep everything *Sabbai Sabbai (Keep everything mellow / relaxed)*.

***

Scott

Hey Kris,

You've never met the chick - that says everything. The fact that she wants to own a bar and she is already calling you babe and baby is telling of her character. Good Thai chicks that want a boyfriend or partner normally do not do this shit. When you Skype with her she's at a bar…that's a big sign right there. If she were a truly decent chick she wouldn't want you to see her at a bar. She's out for the score, whether it be by getting you to marry her, be her boyfriend, or whatever, believe me, there will come a time when she expects money.

Most bar girls are never different. Money comes first, before love or anything and if the money goes, so goes the girl with it. Most bar girls want money in exchange for sex and if you remember this equation, you'll rarely go wrong. So for you, a newbie, there are no exceptions. You don't need a farm girl who needs money and your support. You know nothing about the culture or the language or the people and you're a guy who is ripe for the taking. If you ever make it to Thailand, I would have fun with her, bang her, but no matter what, do not commit.

You're 21 years old and you say you have a lot of sexual experience. Buddy, many foreigners here have been with hundreds and thousands of women and this is no exaggeration. You are a babe in the woods. Like I said, have fun with the chick, but give her NOTHING. Giving your time should be more than enough. My guess is you will eventually shower her with gifts, but this is something men often do here.

As young as you are, you could easily swoop on

some young, cute decent Thai chick. The last thing you need is some Isaan chick in need of a better life.

You say you have gotten rid of all of your animal urges. You are only 21, is there something wrong with you? I've done just about everything a man could want to do with women, I'm 54 and although I've slowed, I still haven't gotten rid of all of mine!

Think about it this way...you meet a chick online and now, after one experience, you are ready to call her a keeper and spend the rest of your life with her? Say what?

If anything, date her and date others for a year or two, get to know the culture, and then, if you really want, make a decision. Do not cave in to her. Use your head and wait until you truly get to know her. All shall be revealed in due time.

BTW, do not tell her what I'm telling you. That would not be very bright.

Scott

***

Kris

Thanks so much for replying.

I exaggerated a little when I said I don't have the animalistic urge to have sex with every woman I see. You know for a fact I probably still have some of that in me. Thanks for the advice Scott; it has helped me a lot.

***

Final Thoughts

One day you turn on the television and see a game of baseball being played.

"Wow, what a fantastic game! I want to play."

Unfortunately, you live in Siberia, freezing your nut sack off, and you can't find anywhere to play or anyone who shares your passion. So you continue to watch the game on TV, dreaming of the day you will finally get to play this magical game. As the months pass, you think more and more about baseball. Then you see the World Series and begin visualizing hitting the series winning home run.

For the time being, you are a fan, nothing more.

Kris is a young man enamored with an exotic, seemingly sweet Thai woman. He's seen his first game of baseball and now needs to put the time in to learn the intricacies of the game.

Instead, he's thinking about winning the World Series with the worst coach in the game.

He's never been to the country, he knows nothing to speak of about Thai women, and despite knowing bar girls are a big no-no, and seeing the signs on the wall, he still feels the need to ask about her character.

How the hell do I know? I am only guessing based on his limited data. I have never met her either. Perhaps he should come to Thailand, have a little fun, and get to know the country.

Notice I made no mention of him meeting the girl? If I thought he was capable of coming here for a week or two without falling head over heels in love, perhaps I would tell him to go see her. I think he's way too immature to be in an overseas relationship with a Thai woman. I don't think he knows his ass from a hole in the wall.

If he does eventually make it to Thailand to visit his online sweetheart, my guess is she'll make mincemeat out of him.

What are the chances she is ready to devote the rest of her life to him?

About the same as making becoming a major league baseball player.

Lenny - Need Dating Advice!

Lenny

Dear Scott,

I am an American living in California who met a Thai woman six months ago on a dating website. She was an *au pair* from Chiang Mai living with a host family here in California. I was not specifically seeking a Thai woman, but she was friendly in our conversations and lived close, so I decided to ask her out. Aside from cultural and language barriers, we seemed to have a good connection and entered into a relationship. As I was doing more research on Thailand's culture, I found your YouTube channel. You did a great job putting things together and I appreciate the work you do. I wish I had found your channel before dating a Thai woman! It would have helped me to gain a little cultural competency I would not otherwise have.

Although my girlfriend seemed to be very nice and a good Thai girl, she had certain inconsistencies that made me suspicious. She scored a three on your *bad Thai girl scale (tattoos, smoking, constantly on her phone). She would get very jealous and suspicious of me whenever we were not together. She would lie on a regular basis about almost anything, which obviously annoyed the hell out of me.

I never really trusted her completely, and I suppose with good reason. Her agency matched her with a new family in Texas and although she wanted to stay in a long distance relationship, I opted to end things amicably. She could have remained in California with me under a tourist visa, but she wanted to continue as an au pair.

As soon as she got to Texas, she began accusing me of all sorts of bad things, spreading rumors to her friends back in California about me to make sure none of them tried to date me after she left. It seems whatever she said about me was working. One by one, many of her friends began blocking me on Facebook, etc., all except for one girl, who I believe had a crush on me. She seems like a more legitimate Thai woman, except for her association with my ex, although to be fair they were just friends through the au pair agency. She is from Nakhon Ratchasima, has no "bad Thai girl" traits, and has a desire to remain in California on a permanent basis. When she learned my ex was moving to Texas, she asked me out. Is this typical behavior or should I be worried? It seemed innocent enough.

The younger Thai generation is more forward than in the past, so I would hardly consider this a big deal.

If I were to pursue things with this woman, I would certainly proceed with extreme caution regardless. Nobody is getting a green card special from me! Ironically enough, I have been going on dates with local women, about a 50/50 mix between white and Asian. I began speaking with another woman who as it turns out is also an au pair from Thailand! She had just ended a relationship with a man in the area because he moved to Texas as well, so we instantly connected and began talking about our intercultural experiences. She is from Buriram and seems to be another very nice girl (zero score on the bad Thai girl scale) although she said she prefers foreign men (even when she lived in Thailand, which half concerns me). My question is what is your knowledge about Thai women who work as au pairs? How do people in Thailand view them? What life situations do they often come from?

Do you have any information about women from Buriram and Nakhon Ratchasima? What kind of questions would you ask these women to get to know them better? I am obviously not going to dive head first into a serious relationship with either of these women, but any advice would be much appreciated!

Lenny

***

Scott

Hi Lenny,

I'll do a video on this—it's too good to pass up. I will definitely change the names of the innocent (and the guilty). You might want to think about staying away from au pair and online relationships though!

All the best,
Scott

***

Lenny

Thanks Scott, I'll be looking forward to seeing what you have to say on the matter. I will include additional background on my situation. Last year I split with my American girlfriend of 10 years which left me somewhat jaded and with lower self esteem.

This is so new school it makes me sick.

"I split with my girlfriend and I am now jaded with low self-esteem."

So he allows her to control how he feels about himself. Gimme a break!

Although the au pair I dated wasn't an angel, I had a great six months of tasty Thai home cooking, fun dates (of which she paid for at least half of the time), lots of great sex, and a chance for my heart and ego to repair itself. I don't regret dating her, but I certainly learned some things along the way.

There is also another factor at play in my involvement with au pair dating. I want to relocate to Canada where I have student status at a very reputable university and better career prospects. The idea of Canada is much more appealing to these women than a typical California girl and arranging a situation that is beneficial to both parties would be a win-win situation. Of course, I could always move up there alone, but bringing a partner has added perks, which I wouldn't mind taking a risk to gain. Worst case scenario would be we part ways in Canada and pursue our goals separately as opposed to me being on the hook for sponsoring someone here in the US. At any rate, I have not, nor do I plan to do anything that I would later regret. I still want to know any information you can provide as it will help me make a better informed decision.

Thanks,
Lenny

***

Scott

Lenny,

I don't fault you—I've done far worse but the whole online, Thai girl thing is something that you ought to use very sparingly and don't give much thought to the women. The only thing that will help is time. Time will show their true nature. Anyone can say anything they want, but it is their actions in the long run that are important. Finding out how a girl got to the US and what their family background is like is important.

Are the girl's parent's farmers or wealthy entrepreneurs? Do they have cars and have money or are they dirt poor. Did she come in to get married or as a student? All this takes time. Worry about yourself, don't move or do anything strictly for a chick, believe that. When I was 19, I moved to California for a girl. She was 16. As soon as I got to California and saw her, her grandparents shipped her ass back to New Mexico where she promptly fell into the arms of some guy who was after her when I was with her. If I had hooked up with her then, at that young age, I would have only experienced a hundredth of what I ended up experiencing in my life. I'm happy she ran off with another guy.

Anyhow...take it easy and good luck.

Scott

***

Lenny

Hey Scott, thanks again.

Let me give you some information about au pairs. The word originates from France and is pronounced *oh pair*. Au pairs are foreign nannies age 18-26 who live with a host family for 6, 9, or 12 months and provide full-time live-in childcare in exchange for a minimum wage salary and an opportunity to have an extended stay in a country they would otherwise not have the funds to visit. Most of the au pairs in California come from Asia, South America, or Europe. Along with providing inexpensive childcare,

Au pairs are required to study English while in the United States. The program is administered by the State Department which authorizes a handful of agencies to recruit, train, and match workers with host families around the country. Au pairs are issued J-1 Visas which can be extended up to an additional 12 months with the same family or a new family. Host families are required to treat their au pairs like a member of the family and give them at least one week of paid vacation, bring their au pair on any family vacations, and give them two days off per week. Upon completing their service to a host family, many au pairs opt to remain in the country on a tourist or student visa, or simply return to their home countries. There are a wide variety of host families choosing to utilize this program, from rich families who wish to expose their children to other cultures to cheapskate families that treat their au pair like slaves. The same can be said about au pair, who can be complete angels or total nightmares, This leads me to the dramatic update I'm about to give you.

Over Labor Day weekend I learned how bat-shit crazy a Thai woman can really get. I was on a lovely date with the woman from Buriram on Friday and we were totally hitting it off. We had a great dinner at a Thai restaurant, and then later I took her to one of my favorite lounges for a drink. I was about to sip my second drink thinking how lucky I was, and to my dismay, in the corner of my eye I see my ex-girlfriend from Chiang Mai! I could not believe my eyes. What the fuck was she doing back in California and how did she end up at the same lounge as us? She was headed right toward our table and that's when I realized holy shit, she followed us here! Since the Thai au pair community in California is small, word got to my ex about who I was dating and she did not take that news well. My date stood up, recognizing my ex, and they started arguing loudly and vigorously in Thai, which I could only imagine translated to something along the lines of "Bitch get off my man" followed by "He's not your man anymore!" A fight broke out, and I kid you not, my ex put my date into a Muay Thai clinch and knocked her out with a blow to the head! My ex's father is a law enforcement officer back in Chiang Mai and trained her to be quite deadly.

Security tackled my ex and called the police. She was arrested for assault and is now in the process of being deported back to Thailand! I feel horrible about the whole situation. My poor date went home with a swollen eye and a bruised ego. I spoke with her yesterday and she is rightfully angry about the whole situation. She knew about my previous relationship with my ex, but I don't think either of us could have predicted it would spin this far out of control. We both agreed to both lay low until my ex is back on a plane to Thailand. I'll send more updates if anything changes.

Laaeow phop gan mai (See you later),
Lenny

***

Scott

Hi Lenny,

I am well aware what an au pair is. I also know there are many, many au pair working in the US who do so illegally for less money than those who are legal. How do I know? Before I came to Thailand, I went out with a French au pair and was also friends with British, Australian and Swedish au pairs.

It doesn't surprise me that your girls did battle. I would have felt terrible for the girl you were with and frankly, I probably would have knocked the girl out who hit her. It's called self-defense or defending someone you are involved with.

It is good to know she's being deported. In Thailand nothing would have happened or she might have paid a little money and that would have been the end of it. As they say here, *som num na or y*ou get what you deserve!

You're playing with fire though and considering there are millions of women out there, there is no need to only go for Thais working as au pair or who you find online. Even though you broke up with her, your previous girl refused to see the truth and thought that if you slept with her, you were her property.

Good luck!

Scott

***

Lenny

Yeah true that... I didn't expect it to get violent, but I think my date underestimated her opponent when she stood up and argued with her. I would have stepped in, but things happened so fast that there wasn't much I could have done to prevent it. If it was my dates' ex boyfriend, you can bet your ass I would have laid him out.

I wasn't aware you knew about au pairs, I got the impression you weren't familiar with them, so I included some information. That doesn't surprise me that nothing would have happened in Thailand from this. My ex would tell me stories of all the times her daddy would get her out of trouble when she screwed up. It looks like she didn't realize that kind of shit doesn't fly here. I guess she's going to be back where she belongs now!

Lenny

Update

Scott

Hi Lenny,
Just wondering, whatever happened with your Thai women?
Let me know if you get the chance.

Thanks,
Scott

***

Lenny

Hey Scott,
Lenny here again! How have you been? It has been a couple years for me and I couldn't be happier. I've been with my new woman for a year and a half now. She is not Thai, ha-ha, and we just got a place together. She's

definitely a better fit than my previous choices in women. I was coming out of a ten year relationship and now that I look back on things, I was on the rebound with the online Thai au pairs. I don't regret my experiences two years ago and I thank you again for your perspective on the matter.

I still have the ability to move to Canada, my friends think that I will do it if Trump gets elected, but I'm not going to let some jackass ruin my life, even if he is president. For the time being, I'm going to stay in California and save money. I am in the process of starting a company. Hopefully it will be successful and if it doesn't pan out, perhaps I'll move north.

If you're curious about what happened to some of the women I spoke of previously, the girl from Chiang Mai avoided deportation and is now illegal somewhere in the US. The nice girl from Korat moved to Australia for a short period and is now back in Thailand. The girl from Buriram moved to Long Island and married a nice Jewish boy, although I think once she got permanent residency has since left him.

I still check up on your channel now and then. I see your perspective has changed on online dating. It is definitely a new day and age, traditional methods of meeting women in public are diminishing because they have their faces buried in their phones.

Cheers,
Lenny

Final Thoughts
Despite what Lenny thinks, my perspective on women has changed very little from when I was in high

school. I still think women should be treated with respect. I still adhere to the man paying for the date, at least in the beginning.

As a teenager and young man in my twenties, I never subscribed to long distance or online relationships and I still believe face-to-face interactions are best when getting to know a woman. Proximity to one another is often regarded as unimportant in getting to know one another on a regular basis. I disagree.

About the only thing that has changed from when I was a teenager is I learned women should not be put on a pedestal unless they have earned the right to be put on one.

Although Lenny had very little trouble landing a woman, this is only a small percentage of the relationship pie. Hooking up with a stable, attractive woman who has her act together takes time; staying with one is more laborious. For whatever reason, whether because of convenience or by design, Lenny had a penchant for au pair and had he said yes instead of no, or zigged when he should have zagged, he might well still be with one who would have made him miserable. Good to know he met someone he gets along well enough to live with.

The bad Thai girl scale

A woman possessing one to four of the following attributes necessitates a much closer look.

1. Constantly asking for money. Do you really want to hook up with Minnie the Moocher?

2. Says all Thai men are no good. Maybe she's the one who is no good.

3. Constantly answering text messages or talking on

the telephone while on a date. While there are exceptions, spending all her time on the phone displays a lack of respect for you and your time together.

4. Regularly uses foul language. I'm referring to the type of woman who curses like a sailor.

5. Spends most of her time in the bar, regularly drinking to excess.

6. Slathered in gold. Tasteful is one thing, doing the Mr. T is tacky and combine with the other attributes is definitely a sign to proceed with extreme caution.

7. Spends money frivolously and yet has non explainable income. If she's spending her money irresponsibly, chances are she'll spend your money irresponsibly as well.

8. Covered in tattoos. Although more Thai young women are getting tattoos, again, combined with the other attributes, you may want to assess whether she fits into your own lifestyle.

9. Smokes. Most decent Thai women do not smoke. Please note—smoking alone does not make her a bad person.

10. Despite never having studied English formally, her English is almost too good. Where did she learn the language? Was she in a relationship with a foreigner? Is she poor? Has she lived abroad?

A combination of these attributes does not necessarily make a bad woman. It should, however, necessitate a closer look at her and the more attributes she has, the greater caution needed. Be sure to give ample time to the relationship, mind you, unpaid time, for her to demonstrate her true motives.

Leo - Old, Fat, Hairy White Men

Leo

Let's be brutally honest here, shall we?

Old, fat, hairy white men who go to Thailand or the Philippines hunting for a wife are looking to buy one. Not literally, of course, but it's still a purchase all the same. It's no different from a rich woman adopting an African child. She doesn't buy the kid, but money changes hands. The woman owns the child in the same way she owns a puppy from the pet store.

So if a Thai girl is going to sell herself to an old, fat, hairy, ugly, white guy, she's gonna get the most money she can out of the deal. Who can blame her when she has to lie down and close her eyes and spread her legs for that? So I have zero sympathy for old, fat, white guys who don't stick with their own kind—old fat white women.

Confucius said it best: "Stay in your lane!"☐

Most real men care very little what other men think about their relationships.

***

Scott

Mister Leo,

Some men do, some men don't and this is where you are mistaken. You stereotype all men who visit or live in Thailand and make no distinction between them. There are a good many foreigners who come to Thailand and the Philippines who have no need to buy a wife.

Before I proceed, do you actually think you are handsome? Because believe me, you have absolutely no room to talk. I looked at your Facebook photos and showed them to a few women; all said, "Not handsome." But of course, you're different, all the girls love you.

I came here when I was young and fit and had no need to pay unless I wanted to do so. But of course, you probably don't believe this because you have never been to Asia. Thus, I dare say your logic and thought process is extremely flawed.

If you actually believe all the older, overweight men in Asia are buying their wives, then you sir are a complete moron. To put it another way, you are a Chowderhead; a dummy, a man with no brains. Did you ever think that maybe some male expats have grown old and gained weight here? Did you ever think that some women might not mind a little meat on their man? How about all the young, strapping, good-looking men who Thai women fall all over—without asking for a single satang?

I know this might be hard to fathom, but I've seen a good number of men here who are fatter and less muscular than me with fine looking women with good jobs who come from good families.

I guess you didn't know this or you are stupid enough to assume otherwise. Perhaps this has something to do with you thinking you know what you're talking about. The truth is you know diddly-squat.

I've been married for 17 years and have lived here for 21. My wife earns as much or more than many people in the US and she certainly doesn't ask me for a monthly allowance to take care of her family. She went to university, graduated, raised our two sons, found a job later on, and has steadily worked her way up the corporate ladder. Our financial arrangement is very much in line with that of most Americans, using our combined income in an effort to reach a common goal good for our family's future.

So I guess I'm just an anomaly, right? Well, not really. I have numerous foreign friends in the same sort of relationships. So while there are certainly fat, ugly men paying their women to be their wives, you lump all men into a single pot. That makes you a Chowderhead. Are you sure you aren't a woman who hates men?

Personally, I don't blame any of the women for anything aside from any deception they put forth. Just because a person has very little money doesn't mean it is acceptable to deceive or steal from another, but of course, you may justify their actions due to their lack of funds. Lemme set your straight pal. 99.99% of Thai women have food on the table and a roof over their head. For some, this is not enough and hard work and honesty carry little value.

So what's different from them than anyone else? We all want a better life. This doesn't mean they need to rob the gullible nor does it mean they all do.

How one chooses to live their life is a matter of choice. Men also have a responsibility to be intelligent with their choices, but most think with the little head as opposed to the big one.

Now Leo...say what you will, but having an Asian woman is much, much different from adopting an

African child. Surely you are more intelligent than this and know the truth. You believe only men who can't get laid back home go to Thailand and if a man has a Thai woman, he must be paying for her. All this and yet you have never even been here! C-H-O-W-D-E-R-H-E-A-D.

If a man has a Thai woman and is paying her outright to be with him, she's a housewife, a whore or a kept woman. It all depends on how you look at it. What I tell men who come here is to find a woman who is capable of earning her own money. For a variety of reasons though, most lack the time or the patience.

***

Leo

Whoa! What a response!

You're right; I have not been to Asia. I had the opportunity to go in 1967, courtesy of the American government, but killing people just for the hell of it is not my thing so I turned the offer down. I am planning a trip to North Korea though.

So this guy is yet another armchair warrior know-it-all.

I have no doubt you have an idyllic situation. A real "The King and I" set up. Great, wonderful, swell, more power to ya.

And yes, I do think that most of those old fat fucks are looking to buy a wife: short term or long term. At least that's true of the ones who get scammed. If they weren't trying to buy her, they wouldn't lose their dough. Right?

Leo has absolutely no problem talking smack about other people, but the truth is, I looked at his photos and

while he was lean, he was nothing an attractive woman would get excited over. He was a wrinkly old man and some might even consider him homely. Of course, his impression of himself is probably different; he probably believes he's every bit as handsome as Brad Pitt or George Clooney.

Not long ago, the Russian mail order bride scam was huge. Some old losers paying $25,000 for what they thought was a young, horny blonde love-slave with big tits from Leningrad. Right!

As for your personal observation regarding moi, I'm still 145 pounds of twisted steel and sex appeal. I wear 30" Wranglers just like I did 50 years ago and I got the rugged outdoor look from living in Arizona all my life. And I have the good sense to stay in my lane. For me, a 40-year-old MILF is robbing the cradle.

'The rugged outdoor look' could also be construed by some (in this case, by me) as old, wrinkly, and having a life that ran him through a meat grinder.

For whatever reason, lately women have been lying to me and telling me they're older than they actually are. So if some chick looks 25 but says she's 40, I ain't exactly checking her driver's license, if you know what I mean. □

Final Thoughts

At the very least, Leo is conceited, not to mention a hypocrite. To him, being with a forty-year-old MILF is robbing the cradle and yet if a chick looks 25 but says she's 40, he 'ain't exactly checking her driver's license.'

There are fat, old, ugly men all over the world, especially in poor countries and some have women that are supposedly out of their league. It happens in the movie business and Rock and Roll all the time. Some of the women are only with the men for their money; others are with them because they're successful or passionate or maybe because he knows how she wants to be treated. Women want men for a variety of reasons. What does it matter though? The men are still with the women, still sleeping with them, having sex with them, and making a life together. It sounds like Leo is jealous.

If a man is paying his way into a woman's heart and panties, then he ought to be intelligent enough to know that if the money goes, the woman goes with it. The highest bidder can have her, unless her desire for money decreases in importance.

What gets me is Leo's conclusions came to him without ever having traveled to Asia. This old coot thinks like a feminist; all men who go to Thailand only go to get laid and all men with Thai women are with them because they can't get women back home. Nonsense, men want to get laid everywhere!

'Stay in your own lane?' Never! Spoken like a true simp.

Confucius lived in a different era and the day a man thinks a woman is out of his league is the day he believes he is less than. Excuse me for pointing this out, but Leo is a pussy.

Everyone gets old and age eventually catches up to everyone. People also tend to gain weight as they grow older. Some people are honest with themselves and some are delusional and truly believe they're 145 pounds of twisted steel and sex appeal. Right and his 40-year-old lady that looks 25 actually find his saggy 70-year-old ass and nut sack a huge turn on.

Lucas - Three Months = 600K Baht

Lucas

Hi Scott,

My name is Lucas and I am 51 years old and live in Sweden. I have read your posts and seen your clips on YouTube. You probably have the experience that I don't.

Brilliant deduction. This is why you are writing me and not the other way around.

I met a fantastic Thai woman in 39 years when I was in Thailand for 3 months. We traveled around together and together we visited her parents' home in Ubon Ratchathani for three days. We are very much in love and it was hard to part with her when I was going home to Sweden. I want to give this relationship a fair chance so we have decided we will build a small house on the land she owns, 100 meters from her parents home.

So nowadays to give a relationship a chance, a man has to build the object of his desire a house prior to getting to know here? Isn't it supposed to be the other way around?

I will give her 600,000 baht and this is almost everything for the house! I've heard about all the incredible stories of wealthy Europeans been cheated. I do not think this is such a story.

Of course not, because his brain isn't working.

I will be traveling back two to three times a year until

I retire and maybe she will come to Sweden a few times. What do you think about the situation? Do you have any good advice to give me?

Sincerely,

Lucas

***

Scott

Honestly, what's the rush? You've known her three months and you are already going to give her 600K baht? Here is my thinking...if you have plenty of money and spending this money won't hurt you one bit, then go for it. But if 600K baht is a large sum for you, then explain this to her. If she is understanding and gives you the time you need to feel more comfortable with the relationship, then you've got a keeper. If she gets upset, then you know she's about the money.

It's amazing how fast Thai women can go from being the love of one's life to wanting to kill you. Perhaps you're right in this case, who knows. She's older, so she may feel like you're a good man, have a little money and you are stable, and thus she isn't out to cheat you. Again, who knows?

You cannot own the land, so even if the house is paid for by you, she owns the land and thus she can make it very, very difficult for you to get the house if the relationship goes into the toilet.

If I were you, I would wait until you've been together for a year and a half to two years before I even considered spending this kind of money.

The two of you will be apart the majority of the time; she will be in Thailand and you will be in Sweden. This means a lot in the beginning of a relationship. You don't know what she'll be doing and you'll have no way of knowing. One way or another though, if you wait to build her a house and she sticks around, perhaps her motives will become more clear.

Hope this helps,
Scott

***

Lucas

Thanks for your opinions. I'll consider them. I know that everything is going fast but when you are in love...

***

Scott

When you're in love, this is the time to think with the big head and not the little one or your emotions. Really, what is the hurry? Are you worried you'll lose her if you don't build her a place? I'd hate to have you come back to me in a few months upset because it didn't work out.

***

Lucas

Never know how this ends. I'm too far away to be retired, but I give this a fair chance.

Final Thoughts

I could have easily called Lucas a Chowderhead. Somehow, I refrained from doing so. Truth is, looking back at this letter; I do think he's an idiot. The success of their relationship requires 600K baht just to start the engine and head down the Yellow Brick Road, what will happen when he is unable to afford something she wants?

When the money goes, she'll go with it and the relationship is over.

First, because he has yet to get to know the woman, second because he's building her a house, and finally, he's building her a house 100 meters from his mother and father-in-law. He lives in Sweden and she'll move in her close family and extended family. When he comes for visits, he'll accept their presence as necessary. Of course, Mom, Dad, Grandma, Grandpa, Auntie, her cousin's cousin and anyone else on the dole will always have their hands out for whiskey, beer, the occasional truck payment, gas money and veterinarian care when the buffalo is sick.

If he is liquid enough to give her 600,000 baht without it causing much damage to his net worth, then who knows, it might be worth the risk. Anything can happen, but I doubt the relationship will have a happy ending. In fact, I think this is a man who desperately wants to believe he and his girlfriend are in love and nothing can go wrong.

Noel - Captain Save-A-Hoe

Noel

G'day Scott,

I have found myself in a bit of trouble after visiting Thailand alone last year. I went for a month in June, then for three weeks from December to January. I need some advice, and I am not sure who else to ask.

To keep it fairly brief, I am from Australia and I am 25 years old. I have been to Thailand on a holiday to Phuket with a group of friends twice before going again alone last year. To be honest, the main reason I wanted to go to Thailand was sex tourism, however, at home I also train in Muay Thai, so I told my friends, family and work that I was going there to train.

I stayed in Bangkok in an apartment I found on AirBnb, trained during the day, then every night I would go out and get a freelancer from Soi 4 or somewhere on Sukhumvit Road. I even ordered a few girls to my room off Craigslist.

Anyway, after spending the first night together, one of these freelancers I paid started coming over to my condo every day. She would bring me food and small gifts and we basically hung out every day for a week after that.

Bam—first mistake—allowing a whore to come over to your condo whenever she pleases.

After I went home to Australia, I stayed in touch with her through Line (a communication app like WhatsApp), and we would regularly message and video call one other multiple times each week. This went on from June until I returned to Thailand in December. She had a Thai boyfriend for a few months in between this time. She did tell me about him so we were unable to speak with each other as often.

I came back to Bangkok in December and the plan was to screw heaps of different girls, train in Muay Thai and travel outside of Bangkok. I was not really even thinking of seeing her. In preparation for the trip, I spent three months learning how to speak and read Thai and I was able to speak a basic level of Thai.

When I got back to Bangkok, she came over to my place and I ended up spending the entire three weeks with her. She stayed with me every day at the condo I was renting. In exchange, she asked me for 1000 baht per day to pay for her bills. She has a year and a half old son staying with her mother and the money went to take care of him and as for her room. We spent every day together and also went to visit her family (her mum, son and her young brother and sister live in Bangkok).

Towards the end of the trip, she came back to my condo with a pregnancy test and told me she was pregnant and I am the father. She told me she can't have an abortion, because she already told her mum she is pregnant and abortion is bad luck in Thailand.

Abortion is never viewed as a positive and no one in their right mind goes into having one done with a smile on their face. But using bad luck is rubbish and falling for this is mistake number two .After all, can an abortion ever be good luck?

She wanted me to go home to her mum's house and

do a sin-sod ceremony where I gave her mum 40,000 baht. Then when I went back home to Australia she wanted me to send her 20,000 baht a month since she can no longer work. She is 19-years-old and had been working as a freelancer on Sukhumvit Soi 4.

I went along with it did the *sin-sod* ceremony and paid the money. Now I am back at home in Australia and she has moved into her mum's house and now is working with her at home. Her mum has a business making clothes, school uniforms, etc.

How about what he wants? Or doesn't this matter? Also, if she could work with her mother at home, why didn't she do so instead of working as a prostitute? Because she has a fish who took the bait and she is going to try and reel him in.

She has shown me paperwork from the doctor that verifies she is pregnant. I do believe she actually is pregnant and I believe she believes I am the father. Her mum even asked for a DNA test, if that means anything, and they also asked me to post a certified copy of my passport which I have done.

Sorry, I would have said no to the certified passport. Knowing how deceitful and scandalous whores can be, the last thing of mine I want them in possession of is a copy of my passport.

I just sent the first 20,000 baht monthly payment to her. Even though on the surface it looks like a scam, I honestly feel like this isn't one.

What do you think Scott? Should I keep sending money? What do I do when the baby is born? What should I do? I have no idea and don't know who to ask. This is really a nightmare. I'm honestly in over my head here mate.

Anyway, I enjoy your videos and hope to hear back from you.

Thanks,
Noel

***

Scott

Noel,

Dude, if you aren't a troll and you actually did this, and then you are a grade-A Chowderhead and not the brightest cat. Think about it...Lemme go to a whorehouse, get involved with a ho, pay her to leave, then I knock her up, DON'T CHECK DNA (she's a whore!) and then I feel the need to give in and pay sin-sod.

Troll = another story like many others.

Non-troll = CHOWDERHEAD who made way too many stupid decisions, all for a little hole.

Good luck,
Scott

***

Noel

Hey Scott,

Thanks for the reply, unfortunately I am not trolling. I am now in the situation where I'm sending her 20,000 baht per month. She is now back living with her mum, unable to work since she is pregnant. The pregnancy is only at six weeks, so I cannot get a DNA test done. I will have to wait until the baby is born.

Her only method of contacting me is through Line,

so I could literally just delete Line and we would have no way of contacting each other. The issue I have is that my own dad ran away before I was born, so I never got to meet him. I have never seen a photo or anything of him and I do not know his name or have any information related to him. My mum died 4 years ago and because of this I can't just run away. Even if there is only a ten percent chance of the baby being mine and a ninety percent chance of this being a scam, if I just deleted her now I would probably always think about whether or not the kid was mine or not for the rest of my life.

Since I have come home, I have been doing heaps of research online about Thai bar girls and reading all the stories of guys getting ripped off, so I know this probably isn't going to end well. I can't just walk away though, because I would have the baby on my conscience.

Also, I am worried that if I stop sending her money she will cut me off from the baby or cut off all contact with me and I will never get to find out if the baby is mine or not.

What do you think I should do Scott?

***

Scott

You still might be able to get a DNA test, but you would need to fly here. Why the hell didn't you do the DNA test right away? That was plain stupid, seriously. You have made some idiotic decisions and now you're going to have to pay for them. If I were you, I would tell your parents if the DNA test shows the kid is yours. Not easy, but necessary, for sure.

I found this information about DNA testing:

A DNA paternity test can be performed accurately before a child is born through amniocentesis, chorionic villus sampling and NON-Invasive prenatal paternity testing (fetal genetic material testing) at between 8 - 13 weeks into the pregnancy.

Why would you delete her though? To me, this is taking the pussy way out. Man up and find out ASAP if the kid is yours. If it's not yours, say goodbye. If it's yours, do what's right. That is, pay and be responsible for sticking your dick in her. Why the hell would you give sin-sod to a whore who already has a child with someone else? Again, this is just plain stupid.

She is unable to work now, while she's pregnant, but mark my words; I wouldn't put it past her to go back to work once the kid is a few months old—even with the 20K a month you are sending her. You got yourself into one helluva pickle and this sort of problem is exactly why I am always saying men should not get seriously involved with bar girls.

Don't put your pecker in any woman if you would not be satisfied making her your girlfriend or wife. Now the only thing to do is cross your fingers and hope she was banging someone else.

Good luck,
Scott

***

Scott

Sorry about telling you to tell your parents. I just remembered what you wrote. That's tough and it's tough not having anyone to turn to about this. But for the good of the child, do the right thing. I think it will be much easier to live with yourself.

Scott

***

Noel

Hi Scott

Thanks for the advice about the prenatal DNA test, I didn't know such a test existed. Can you recommend a hospital or clinic in Bangkok that can do this procedure? I emailed Bumrungrad International Hospital asking the test, but they sent me a generic response about a standard DNA testing. I would need to make an appointment with the mother and child.

When I did a Google search for Prenatal DNA Test in Bangkok, I could not find any trustworthy looking places. Should I just email all the big hospitals in Bangkok?

I am planning on coming back to Bangkok for a week in June to get this test done. This is the earliest I can get time off work; otherwise I'll be constantly stressed out for the next nine-plus months not knowing if I am the father or not.

Thanks again for your help,

Noel

***

Noel

Hi Scott,

Last week, I emailed every major hospital in Bangkok, enquiring about prenatal DNA testing. I contacted Samitivej, Bumrungrad, plus a few more, and I even got in contact with the Police General Hospital

Forensic Department through Facebook messenger. None of these places offer prenatal testing.

The only place I can find online that offers prenatal testing is PTC Labs Thailand. The test is 47,900 baht. The question I have is do you know of a reliable hospital or lab in Bangkok where I can get this test? I don't know if PTC Labs is legit or not.

How exactly am I going to determine this? It would seem to me that any place setting themselves up to do these tests should be visited by Noel. Seems like a helluva lot of work, but in his situation, I think it's warranted.

Currently, I am sending 20,000 baht per month, so if the prenatal test is 47,900 baht, is it worth getting the test done ASAP or should I wait until the baby is born and I can get a standard paternity test for 15,000 baht? To get the test done as soon as possible I would have to take a week or two off work unpaid, pay for expenses to go to Thailand plus pay for the DNA test. It would cost me nearly $5000 Australian to do all this.

This is how it goes. If he's dead set on making sure she is indeed pregnant with his child and he wants to do what he views as the right thing, it's gonna cost him. The only way around this is bailing on her and he's already stated he did not wish to do this.

Currently, she is messaging me on Line every day and we video call for 10-20 minutes per night, every night without fail. She is constantly telling me she loves me, she misses me, please come back, etc. The whole situation is getting pretty frustrating, because I do not have any feelings for her, I just want to find out if this baby is real and if it is mine or not.

If Liam had a friend or family member in Thailand, he could have easily had the girl take a pregnancy test at a local hospital. If she declined to take a test, he would have known she was scamming him and this would have been the end of his dilemma.

I know all she wants out of me is money, so we are both pretending to like each other, constantly messaging and video calling. She is just pretending to love and miss me for the money and I am just staying in touch with her in case we are really having a baby together.

A couple of weeks ago I had enough of this whole thing and messaged her.

"Am I just a customer? I know you just need money for your family," etc. We did a video call and she was crying and hyperventilating, saying before I was just a customer, but now we are having a baby together and she loves me. After I met her for the first time in June of last year, we stayed in touch for 5-6 months, messaging and video calling several times per week. Then she basically told me I only viewed her as a prostitute.

Despite her wanting Liam to believe she is some poor, destitute girl from a downtrodden family, she is indeed prostitute! She made her bed and now she is laying in it.

After this I just feel sorry for her. She has to provide money for her mum and son and her young brother and sister and the only way she has to do this is to prostitute herself. What is really worse than having sex for money is she has to create fake relationships where she pretends she loves someone and has a baby with someone, all for her family's financial security.

Okay, it's sad. This is life. There are sad and

terrible things occurring all over the world. There are
also men and women saying and doing anything to
make a buck. Some truly have no options, like children
sold into prostitution by their parents and others simply
have options they do not like or do not wish to
entertain.

That being said, I have no interest in being her
Captain Save-A-Hoe, but now I feel like I should just
send her the money every month, keep her happy by
messaging and video calling with her.

Noel

***

Scott

Noel,

I need a day or two to check everything out and also
to think about this. At this point, it's not about being a
Chowderhead or what you did in the past; it's about the
child and whether or not it's yours. I can assure you I
view this as a very serious issue…To me, leaving a
woman and not taking care of the child is
unfathomable…you wanna pay, you gotta play. Listen to
some of the knuckleheads on YouTube and they will tell
you to leave—but this is a decision that will affect you
and the woman and the child for your entire lives. So
indeed, it is serious.

Some of what you wrote, like her saying you think of
her as a prostitute, is inevitable. Personally, I think
honesty is the best policy, however, have you tried
telling her (and lying about this) that you are flying over
for a DNA test in the next week or two and listening to
and see her reaction to this? If she's okay with it, my

guess is it might just be yours. I wouldn't, however, believe her crocodile tears. This is the thing about being a prostitute—once a man is paying for their body, it becomes hard to believe anything she says is related to anything other than the money. She is young, and if she didn't already have one child I might be more apt to believe her, but she already has one kid, who knows what went on with the father. Now at 19, she's already worked as a prostitute and has a second kid on the way. No matter how you slice it, this is not good.

There is a difference between doing your part to make sure the child is okay and taking care of her. I know it sounds harsh, but you aren't obligated by anything other than your own morals. Legally, you're free and clear if you want it, but until you find out if you are the father, you'll always wonder if you father a child with some prostitute you made a mistake with.

Like I said before though, this is a perfect example of why men need to use a condom and refrain from getting into any sort of relationship other than pay and go.

Keep your head up...
Scott

***

Noel,

Thanks Scott,
I think I will try the trick you said about telling her I am flying over for the DNA test to see how she reacts.

***

Noel

Hi Scott,

197

Tonight when we spoke she was asked me when I was coming back and I said June. Then she coincidentally brought up doing a DNA test. We discussed her getting one done when we first found out she was pregnant. She said that the DNA test can also tell if the baby is a boy or girl, so it sounds like she has been doing her research. She also said that after the DNA test she wants to go to the Amphur (District Administrator) and change her surname to my surname.

What does this mean? Is she talking about getting married? I was planning on bringing up the DNA test to see how she reacted as you suggested and then she just randomly brought it up.

I suggested a few weeks ago that she start going to high school. I read online there are Sunday schools for adults who left school at a young age. This school allows them to finish *Mattayom 6* (High School). I also suggested she learn English. She brought up that she wants to start going now because she has time while she is pregnant. Apparently there is a program near her place that starts in a couple of months.

Noel

***

Scott

Noel,

She wants to get married, perhaps for the kid or perhaps because she thinks you'll stick around. Who knows? I gotta say…if you aren't in love with her, then everything is for the kid. If there's any chance you want to be with her, again, this is another example. This time, it's about trust. You can't trust her, you aren't sure of her motivations, so why on earth would anyone want to get involved in this sort of relationship? Anyhow, what's done is done. Personally, and obviously if you have the money, I would want to know NOW if the child is yours or not. I wouldn't want to go through the hell of waiting. Maybe she's telling the truth, but somehow you need to tell her that it's not her, it's that she was working in a bar and she's just not the girl you want to spend the rest of your life with. Try not to upset her, if not for any other reason than she's pregnant, but her profession, for whatever reason, makes it difficult for you to trust her in such a difficult situation. You don't want her hyperventilating…

She probably isn't going to care about what you say about it not being personal and she might get emotional, but it needs to be out in the open.

If the child is yours, then if possible, you need to try and provide for the child *and* if possible, put her in a position where she can provide for herself. Going back to school, English school, whatever…you're in a terrible spot, but you just need to forge ahead and deal with each issue until everything is somewhat resolved.

Scott

***

Noel

Hey Scott,

I have a new update as of today/yesterday. In the last month, I have sent a total of about 35,000 baht. I found an English teacher to tutor her in English; 20 hours for 7500 baht. I set up a meeting between her and the teacher and sent the payment. This is in addition to the

20,000 baht monthly payment. Also, she said she had to give all her money to her mum so she asked me for another 5000 for herself. Then on Saturday she wanted another 3000 to buy clothes because she has gained weight.

The requests will only end when all his money is gone or he completely breaks it off.

Anyway, I just want a clear conscience from this situation so I am sending the money. However, this is 35000 baht, which is over 1000 Australian dollars. Before, I was able to save just over 1k Australian per month. Now I am sending her all this money and I can save nothing. All I can do is pay my bills, so it's been pretty stressful thinking about what I am going to do in the future since I'm unable to save any money.

On Sunday, she changed her Line profile photo and cover photo. These were pictures of me and her and pictures of her son. I wondered what was up. I thought she was angry at me or something, but I talked to her about it on video chat and she seemed fine.

Anyway, fast forward to yesterday. Normally during the day while I am at work she messages me on Line, but yesterday she didn't, so I wondered what was up. I am not friends with her on Facebook because I barely use Facebook now, but I knew her name on Facebook so I can search her and see her profile picture and cover photo. She had changed her Facebook cover photo from a picture of us to just a picture of a tattoo of Google images.

I looked at who had liked one of the photos. It only had six likes, but one of the people who had liked the photo had a profile picture of a Thai guy and *her* naked in bed together. She was smiling. I recognized the guy as her boyfriend from last year. I knew it was a recent picture because of her hair and her necklace.

Anyway, she didn't call or message me at all yesterday and it wasn't until today after work that she messaged me saying that she had a problem with her mum and she couldn't go home.

Then I sent her the screenshot of her and her Thai boyfriend together.

Then I sent her a message, "He made you pregnant, not me!"

Her response was "I'm sorry for everything."

I think what happened is she found out she was pregnant when we were together in December. She knew either I or her Thai boyfriend made her pregnant, so she spoke to her mum and her friend Jum, who is in her thirties, or they advised her to convince me the baby was mine to get money.

What does it matter why she did what she did or if someone else advised her?

It is a pretty weird situation, because she had photos of me and her on her Facebook that I could see from last year before she made her profile private. I could see everything she posted. So she was putting photos of me on her Facebook, not knowing that I could see them, captioning them with 'I miss you,' etc., in Thai. She also had photos of the sin sod ceremony that had over 150 likes. All her friends on Facebook were congratulating her. This is unreal. Is everyone in Thailand in on scamming foreigners?

No, definitely not all Thais, but those expecting a whore to have scruples are asking for trouble.

She also talked about what features of mine she wanted our baby to have. A big thing for her was she wanted to have a nose bridge that sticks out. The Isaan Thais have flat nose bridges as you would know; she even got a silicone nose bridge implant put in because she didn't like hers.

I think she really isn't sure who the father is out of me or her Thai boyfriend. She loves him but I am obviously the much better financial option.

Obviously I feel like a dickhead for getting sucked into the most obvious scam. I was even sort of looking forward to having a baby, however sending all that money over there was getting very stressful. I now feel so relieved. I have some plans for the future which require me to save money so now I can continue doing so.

Scott, what should I do from here? I am thinking the best thing is just to block her, but I should still make sure she has my Line ID or email address or some way of contacting me. This way, if the baby comes out looking half *farang*, she can contact me and I will go back and have her do a DNA test.

I really do not want to have any further contact with her unless the baby turns out to be mine because to be honest, I developed feelings for her. I have been in regular contact with her (multiple times a week) since June of last year when we first met and the last few months we've been messaging and video calling every single day. So she became a part of my life and I looked forward to her calls and messages.

Noel

***

Scott

Hi Noel,

After seeing her on Facebook with another dude, naked, that's all she wrote. She's a whore and despite any guilt you may have felt, an unwanted pregnancy of any kind is part of her business. Tough shit. No DNA test, she should not get one satang more and I would definitely block her ass from all methods of communicating. If ever the day comes where a kid comes to you and says you're his father, you can deal with it then. At this point though, cut your losses and let her fuck off back into her world.

Scott

Final Thoughts

This is a troubling conversation for several reasons. First and foremost, because there is a baby involved and if Noel decided to split, the baby will eventually grow up wondering why his father wasn't around and this can and probably would have serious long-term consequences. Next, not only is Noel is foolish enough to get emotionally involved with a bar girl, he also had sex with her sans condom *and* then supposedly knocked her up.

Although Noel pissed away a fair chunk of money to this girl, he could have been much worse off. He could have been paying for the next 18-plus years. He screwed up, learned a hard lesson, paid his dues, and hopefully he learned from his mistakes.

Trusting your gut instinct often is difficult to do when faced with no-win situations like this one. More than likely had Noel been less compassionate, less of a Captain Save-a-Hoe and less troubled by his father leaving him when he was young, it would have been easier for him to tell the girl to get lost. Coulda, shoulda, woulda...

Remember the Golden Rule—do not get emotionally involved with a bar girl (or any other form of prostitute).

Noel's situation is *exactly* why men need to pay and go when using a prostitute. If a man is stupid enough to get into a relationship of any kind with a prostitute or any other woman, at least in the beginning, use some form of birth control, preferably a condom. Using a condom sucks, but it's better than the alternative. The girls can be so sweet and sexy and convincing, but the idea to get across to men is to keep their wits and remember if they're sleeping with someone they barely know and not using a condom, the consequences can be severe.

Oliver - Money, Money, Money

Oliver

Hi Scott,

I stumbled on some of your videos on YouTube and really liked them. You don't pull any punches with what you say and they definitely hit home.

Just wanted to run something past you, which I sort of already know the answer to.

I was in Thailand March 2014 and met a girl from Phuket. She was a working girl from a massage parlor and she has a daughter who stays with her parents in Chachoengsao, outside of Bangkok. Just so you know, I didn't get asked if I wanted any extras.

While Thai women working as traditional masseuses can and often are simply there to give massages sans hanky-panky, with a bit of cajoling, many are willing to provide on-site and after hours extras. So before we go declaring her an angel, let's slow down and remember that in time, all shall be revealed.

Not the best situation, I know, but I asked her out for a drink after she finished work because she looked cute and spoke pretty good English. I spent the next couple of weeks with her on and off due to her working, but she came to see me and spent a fair bit of time with me. She didn't even go to work a couple of days to spend them with me. Standard stuff it seems, but what got me thinking was that she didn't ask for any money from me. Obviously, I bought her food and drinks, but that was it.

I am 38 in good shape as I go gym and train in Muay Thai and I am decent looking. I dress trendy and I look after myself. She's 29, so I thought our situation was not the typical old-guy, young-girl scenario and maybe she does actually like me.

Right, his situation is different. She is different. Here we go! Is he the only guy who thinks himself handsome and young enough for a younger woman? There is a nine year age difference. Is this really so uncommon? Please...

Anyway, I went home and she went back to her village to spend time with her daughter, but we kept in touch via WeChat over the next couple of months. It was the odd couple of messages each day. She then had to go back to Bangkok to work and the messages increased, which I put down to her having more free time.

Why would this woman have more free time when she is working full-time? Did he ever think that maybe she was going to visit her Thai husband or boyfriend? It should not have mattered though, what he should have done was had his fun with her and move on.

My motive to stay in touch was because I got on well with her on holiday and thought it would be nice to meet up again when in Thailand.

Another mistake, for if he was really so desperate to see her again—which he shouldn't have been—he should have gone home, forgotten her, and then when he went back to Thailand, gone back to the same place.

One day she told me she had something serious to say to me, but couldn't yet. I was obviously wondering what it was and it took her a further three days until she did tell me. I am going to assume that the following is a scam, but one I have not heard about before. What she basically said was that a year before she met me, she met a German guy. He has met with her three times. The last time he went to her village to see her parents and asked her mum if he could marry her. Supposedly, he had given her parents 250,000 baht to marry her. She told me in Phuket that she didn't have a boyfriend or a guy, so that's one lie, but to cover that, she said she didn't expect to like me so much and in her heart she knows that I am the right one for her, not this other guy. Straight away I thought it was a scam, but I wanted to see how things unfolded just to be sure.

If there is too much drama right from the outset, then the relationship is probably not worth it. In this case, why would a British man get involved with a poor Thai woman he has little in common with and who has already started with the drama?

Also, when a Thai woman gets married, the money is given at the wedding, not months prior. This way the money can be displayed for friends, family and neighbors to see. The more money, the more face the family gains.

She said she has created a big problem for her family and she is worried about this guy who paid the money. I simply asked where the money had gone and she told me that maybe her parents have some, but not all, and that's when I got the impression she was hinting at me paying her way out of this problem.

So what does this say? Time to wake up Chowderhead!

The things that followed didn't add up to me. She told the German guy she was having second thoughts about marriage and apparently he was okay with this.

I asked if he wanted his money back and she said he never mentioned it. When I told her I didn't believed he would give in so easily, she kicked off and got the hump with me saying I don't believe her.

This is where Oliver could and should have ignored this financial matter. No questions, no comments, it is time to change the subject.

"Sorry, the rice is burning, I gotta go."

If the situation is real, it's her problem. She got herself into the situation; she can get herself out of it.

A short time later, this settled down and she was back to saying nice things to me. Then she tells me she has spoken to her parents and they think she's a crazy girl, but it didn't seem to be as a big an issue as she first presented.

Seems a little convenient to me.

I didn't say too much and never gave the hint that I would give any money over and she just messaged as normal for the next couple of days. I was just waiting for the money thing to come up again and sure enough it did. She said that out of the blue the German told her he wants his money back. I asked how can she do this and she said the parents have 180,000 out of the 260,000 he gave them, so they were 80,000 baht short.

When I didn't offer any help, she said things like, "It's okay, you don't have to help me," and "I just want to go somewhere far away." Basically she was just kicking off because she wasn't getting her own way, or so it seemed.

As soon as she started in with this bullshit, he should have told her he had things to go and couldn't talk. No more answering her calls. No more relationship. End of story.

"Bye-bye honey, take good care of yourself."

But no, he had to prolong their romance, of course.

Since then, it has been and up and down. One day she is happy, saying nice things to me like she misses me and wants to come to England to stay with me and then the next day, she is moody, with short, curt messages. She is sometimes nasty and often has a go at me. She seems to always turn around innocent things I say, making out like I am the one at fault. It almost seems like she sets it up to have a-go at me.

If it looks like a duck and walks like a duck, it's a duck. She is doing everything she knows to manipulate him and yet he continues the relationship.

She told me that at the end of the month she was vacating her room and putting her belongings in her sister's room, so I asked where she was going to stay. She said with friends, but then added "Do you think I am staying with someone else? With a man?"

I told her no, I was simply asking. This sort of thing became common whereas before when I spoke to her she was really nice.

It's funny how things have taken a downhill spiral after mentioning the big problem of the German who supposedly paid her family to marry her. The relationship has gotten worse, possibly due to the fact that I haven't offered to pay anything.

I can only assume it's a scam to get money and probably stems from the people she is working with in the scene she does.

Does it really matter why she is trying to scam him? Have your fun, get on down the road and remain in control of the relationship. Never let a woman like this pressure or manipulate you. At best, it's a waste of time, at worst; it might cost a man everything he has.

It would be nice to get your thoughts on this. I know you must be a busy guy and probably sick and tired of the subject of girls and *farang* in Thailand, but I like to think I am one of the more sensible ones.

Say what? Is he delusional?

I can see how people do get sucked into all this. Thailand is a magical place, but you have to use your head over everything else or you will encounter some serious problems.

All the best
Oliver

***

Scott

Hello Oliver,

Why on earth would you want this chick? If you're as sensible as you say you are, you should have just screwed her and forgotten her. She's a liar driven purely by money and you don't know what's true and what's not. Just reading this nonsense has me dizzy. Find a girl who has a decent job and who isn't desperate and if possible, who doesn't have a child. It doesn't matter if a girl is working in a massage parlor with or without extras; hook up with the owner of the massage parlor, not the worker. At least then she might actually have some money. The worker in a massage parlor is going to inevitably be poor and thus, in need of your money, as opposed to wanting to be with you because handsome, dapper and charming.

From my own experience, I have been to several massage parlors where happy endings were not allowed, however, I got the girl's phone number and then later that night or the following night she was in my bed within minutes of her arrival.

I remember the last girl quite well. She kept telling me how much she liked me. Then when it was time for her to leave, I asked if she wanted money.

"Yes, of course," she said. "How much you give me?"

She liked me, but she wanted and liked the money more.

If there's always drama and urgency, you are better off alone or in a healthier relationship. If you really value my advice, hear me. Life is too short, who needs the aggravation? Don't just listen or read the words, allow them to sink in. I wouldn't have given your girl the time of day after I got what I wanted. As blunt as this seems, she also got what she wanted, M-O-N-E-Y (at least for the massage).

If she's been with one foreigner already and she's trying to hook up with you, what does that tell you? She's working at a massage parlor, which is like working in a bar. There are Thai and foreign customers going there all day, every day. My guess is you and the German are not the only one's she's been with or attempted to extract money from.

She's a *farang* chaser, which means she's chasing the dough, the Golden Ticket, the Walking ATM; she's in search of the pot of gold at the end of the rainbow. How about you find one who doesn't need your money and wants to be with you for what you have to offer as a person? How about you find one who earns her own money? How about you both work on building your financial portfolio together like people in normal relationships? This isn't as easy, but at least the majority of your conversations won't only be about money and other men.

Good luck,
Scott

***

Oliver

Thanks Scott,

I really appreciate the reply and it is pretty much what I thought. You get sucked into the fact that the girl is cute and we did get on really well together, but I suppose anyone can act however they need to for two weeks. The urgency thing did set off alarm bells and I sort of think she was trying to get me to pay that full *sin-sod* money of 250,000 baht. When I didn't pay up, she got the hump and then reassessed the situation and attempted to get a lesser amount.

I have read so many stories on the net of people being ripped off, but I won't pay anything. I have even read that a westerner should not have to pay *sin-sod* because it's a Thai tradition. But if he does, the fact the girl has a daughter should cancel it out.

I am planning on moving to Thailand at some point and I am of two minds as far as the best way to go. The first route would be to save up some cash over the next year so I can maybe have about 20,000 British Pounds. I would rent my house out and go over for a year an educational visa, but look for work while there. I am a graphic designer, so ideally some work in this field would be ideal. The place I really like is Phuket and my plan was to live in Kathu or Phuket Town. This may cut down my options for work.

Definitely.

The second route is to pay off my mortgage over the next four or five years, then rent it out and move to Thailand. The money from the rent would give me enough to live on in Thailand without needing to work.

The first route means I can go out sooner and at a younger age, but if things don't work out with finding a job, my 20K would keep me there for two years, but then I would have to return to the UK.

The second route means I could stay in Thailand without the worry of needing to come back to the UK due to not needing to find work. The downside is that I would be a few years older and a lot can happen in five years.

Thanks again Scott, I value your wise words.

Regards,
Oliver

Final Thoughts

Why do so many men seem to hear what I am saying, yet most never truly listen and act accordingly?

Men have been sucked in by women's sexuality from the beginning of time and foreign men have been falling in love with Thai women since before the Vietnam War. Maybe it's about time they realized they need to read between the lines and think with the big head.

If more men visiting or living in Thailand took their

time instead of rushing in to a relationship, there would be less men would be writing me. My guess is there will never be a shortage of gullible, inexperienced, foolish Chowderheads in need of relationship advice. Better them than me.

Patrick - The Pattaya Dilemma

Patrick

Hi Scott,
I have been watching a helluva lot of your YouTube videos and would like to ask you a few questions, but I am not sure if you reply to many messages from people as you probably have a heap to reply to. This is the only place I am thinking I can ask. I suppose I will just wait to see if you reply to me on this message before I post another to you.

Anyway, I think your opinions are tops.

Cheers matey.
Patrick

The preamble is so unnecessary. Just ask the question already and if I answer, I answer, if I don't, I don't.

***

Scott

What do you need to know?

***

Patrick

Hi Scott,
I have a few questions, so I'll ask one for now.
Again with the preamble! Get to it already! It's

215

taken this guy 108 words to tell me he wants to ask question. Just ask the question!

Right, so I am planning to go back to Pattaya in October of this year. I have not been able to go for three years now because I got hooked up here in Melbourne with a *farang* lady, a jealous *farang* lady at best. She let me go to Thailand alone three times while I was with her and one condition of our relationship from the very start was to not stop me from going. Well, after three trips she stopped me and made my life hell here.

Gee, I wonder why?

Now I have long split from her and I am now seeing a Thai woman from Thailand.

Is it any wonder there are so many bitter Thai women?

She has never been a bar girl and has only worked in a restaurant in Thailand. She is doing the same thing here in Australia. The relationship is all good and she doesn't mind me going alone to Thailand one time per year. I am taking the chance with this one as I want to stay with her.

A man and woman part ways. He decides to move on and in no time at all, he's back on the prowl. Sure enough, super-stud that he is, he meets a lovely Thai woman he wants to stay with. He just needs to make sure his dream girl will ALLOW him to travel to Thailand to bang as many whores as he can.

*"Why not, honey, all I want is for you to be happy,"
she says, gleefully.*

Now, the Pattaya dilemma; I recently reactivated my Facebook account that I had deactivated three years ago. My Thai friends from the bars where I used to hang out have all come flooding back now. They know exactly when I am coming. In particular, there is one girl who was my girl for a couple of nights here and there the last time I was there. She has since moved on with some old Swedish guy who travels back and forth to Thailand to see her every so often. He also comes to check on the house he is building her in Buriram. She wants me to go to Korat or Surin to meet her and have a good time as she has promised the Swede won't find out. Supposedly, I am the only special guy she has kept in touch with since she left the bar. I do not believe her, but she just sounds so bloody well genuine about wanting to see me.

If I do see her up there, I don't want my only holiday for three years turning to shit because of some Swedish guy, Also, I don't want to be with her if three or four days into our time together she has a phone call from him telling her to go back home.

Sounds to me as if he's madly in love with his Thai girl in Australia! True love!

I do like this girl, but I have been to Thailand 16 times before and don't want to get stung. She is not asking me for any money, but keeps hinting that her smart phone is broken.

Thanks for reading and any comments would be great,

Cheers,
Patrick

P.S. The other thing I need to get an opinion on is that this time I am going to have a real tight budget of around 4500 baht per day in Pattaya. Try hotel is already paid for and the 4500 baht does not include this. I am not into go-go bars, just beer bars. A lot of guys on the Thailand forums are 50/50 on whether or not this is enough. Some say don't bother going, some say it can be done as long as I stay out of go-go bars. What is your view on this?

My view is he has no brains.

Bar fines at beer bars are still only 300 and to go long-time with them is between 1000 and 1500 baht.

Cheers,
Patrick

***

Scott

So…lemme get this straight pal, you're hooked up with a Thai girl in Oz who you want to stay with, but you're coming to Thailand to see some slut. She has a boyfriend, a boyfriend who is building her a house and of course, this makes no difference to you or to her.

Sounds way too messy to me, after all, if you're gonna fool around on your girl in Oz, don't you think there are other less problematic women in Thailand you can run around with? If you go whoring in Pattaya, you can just pay them to go away. No muss, no fuss.

Going up to Korat or Surin, seems like a waste of time. If it were me, I'd be strong enough to look around for new women, women who don't have some foreign husband or baggage.

My suggestion is you have a tad bit of integrity and stay away from the chick. Sounds to me like way to much hassle for a piece of ass.

Another rule I have—don't travel for the pussy! Seems like a huge pain in the ass just to come see some whore you took before. Especially since she is already taken.

If you can't get by on 4500 baht a day, something's wrong with you. Budget your money and stay within the 4500. Not all that difficult...unless you're going out getting drunk every night and going nuts. If you have a little self-control you shouldn't have any problem.

And remember, Karma is a bitch.

Scott

***

Patrick

Thanks heaps for the heads up. You have a very straight and logical view of things. This is why I follow you on YouTube.

Cheers,
Patrick

Final Thoughts

Thailand attracts idiots and Patrick is a perfect example of this. In addition to being a Chowderhead, he is a man who allows himself to be controlled by women and who has no control over his finances. One of these faults is bad enough; the combination illustrates his lack of control in his own life.

His airfare and hotel are paid for and if he stays in Pattaya, transportation is cheap, even free if he chooses to use his own two feet to get around.

He has a whore who says she tells him, "Mr. Patrick, you number one for me," and he thinks this is a big deal. She's got a husband, he has a girlfriend he says he wants to stay with, and instead of forgetting the whores, or in his case, a whore, he is willing to travel all the way back to Thailand just to put his pecker in her a few times.

Patrick says he doesn't believe what this girl says, but my guess is he is head over heels in love with her, or at least the thought of her and he believes her when she tells him he's special! Yes, Mr. Patrick, you are the chosen one. Her Swede is old and ugly, not to mention stupid, he has a tiny penis can't get it up and he never makes her cum.

The truth is she is looking for a sponsor or companionship; the truth is she's a snake who is cheating on her boyfriend. He probably has a huge cock, makes her feel insecure, gives her more money than he should (which she squanders) and is a great guy.

Patrick could come to Thailand, sleep with a few different women, go home, and hopefully, live happily ever after. Instead, he lacks self-control and allows his pecker to lead him into turmoil. He is a major-league Chowderhead, no doubt about it.

Peter - Is My Girl Different?

Peter

Hey Scott,
I can imagine you get a lot of messages, I just watched a bunch of your videos, and having done this, I would like to share a story and see whether you possibly could provide some feedback. I feel a bit stupid, although, I am a strictly professional person with wide open eyes and might already know what you would say if you were to reply. I have been to a Bangkok a couple of times and while there, I met this girl, ironically enough in a bar. I was drunk and ended up taking her home.

The next day we exchanged phone numbers and I continued my holiday, traveling to Phuket. I kept in touch with her. We did the usual things, like seeing the sites, trying different foods and laughing and joking with one another. She was super friendly and helpful and there was no catch on meeting up again or anything like that. When I returned to Bangkok, I went with a mate who has been living in Bangkok for a couple of years and we passed by the bar where I met her. Ironically, I ended up talking with her again, my friend left, and after a couple of hours I left with her for a drink. After this, we went back to my hotel, only this time I gave her no money.

Right…isn't it ironic?

Let me give you some info on myself. I have never had any problems with girls or getting attention and for my age (25). I have been with many girls (40+) as well as in relationships ranging from my own age up to 35.

I never felt such strong chemistry with anyone like I did with this girl, physically and with our ability to laugh together. I stayed in touch with her over the next 3-4 months, no strain, just more of the same thing, laughing and joking on a friendly level.

I was working abroad in China, Spain and Switzerland and then I received a surprise promotion and was asked to move from China to work in Thailand. This occurred without requesting it and it had nothing to do with this girl. I promised myself I wouldn't tell her anything, but one week before heading back to Europe for my working visa, I told her I had received a new posting in Phuket and I would be stopping in Bangkok. I arranged for a formal date, because I wanted to see for myself if my feelings for her were just stupid, blind feelings from before. This time she asked if she could stay with me in the hotel since we arranged to go on a formal date and I carefully invited her. We had a great time. While heading back we started having a really intense connection.

I already have a feeling this guy is a sucker. He carefully invited her?

She's a bar girl and he can't keep himself away from her. Of course, she asked him if she could stay with him at his hotel (since they were going on a formal date and he carefully invited her) and of course, he said yes!

Obviously his feelings were stupid and blind. That's

what she was counting on!

Now after living in Thailand for about one month, everything was still the same. She was constantly telling me she misses hanging out with me and that I made her feel special, but neither of us have spoken of love.

To give you some info on her, she is 28 and is from Isaan. She told me her story.

At 17, she was forced into a marriage, had a kid, and then divorced.

Right, she was forced. While possible, I doubt it. Call it a hunch.

She no longer is in contact with her previous husband. Because of this, she is also no longer on speaking terms with her father.

She started working in a factory, and then later on, she began working as a masseuse and then moved to Korea doing the same thing. After this she worked in Malaysia and she continued on this road until she became a bar girl in Bangkok. She said her reason for doing so was because her parents had expenses and she was expected to cover them.

Already this is way too drama for my taste and just reading her story is enough to turn me off. A woman who is divorced, has a kid, and has traveled to Korea and Malaysia to work as a masseuse—more than likely giving happy endings—has more than her share of baggage. In my world she could only rise to the status of friend, or friend with benefits, but she would never rise any higher.

I am not sure what a girl like this makes per month. I have been clear in that I would only help her with advice. After that first night, she never asked me for money or to pay for anything. I would never ask her to change unless she would change herself. However, she is telling me that she is looking to do something different. She is telling me that she does what she is doing in order to support her parents as her brother does nothing and her sister is also a masseuse.

She had a Swedish boyfriend for a period of time and tried living in Sweden, however she moved back to Bangkok after 3-4 months. She told me she moved back because she just could not get used to her new life there. Sweden is cold and she got lonely as the guy would spend most of the time working. Plus she could not speak the language.

Like I said, way too much drama! Why not just take your time and find a girl who has less baggage? This is a perfect example of a guy thinking with his emotions or the little head instead of the big one.

To be clear, over the last five months I have talked to her every single day, either through instant messaging, phone or Skype, however, I cannot say that I know her since we have only met for about seven days effective time. Sometimes she would spend her days off talking to me on Skype for up to ten hours. I have never done this with anyone, ever. I have always been very clear towards her that I would not give her anything except me and despite this she has continued talking to me in the same way.

Recently, she went back to her hometown, something she does once a year. She has been saving money over the last year to change her ways and open her own small shop. She told me she would be able to do this sometime soon and like I said, she has never asked me for any money for this or anything else. What she has been asking me about is about self-motivation, how to become successful professionally and tips and opinions on her thoughts. The only change when she went back home is we instant messaged more and spoke less over the phone. However, she kept telling me that she would like to tell me something positive the next time we spoke regarding her own life.

I have given her two gifts; one bracelet worth 200 baht with a note when I met her the second trip and a bottle of perfume from the duty free the last time I saw her. That's as far as I would stretch. I am not asking you whether these circumstances justify making her my girlfriend, because I am not looking for that, however I would like your opinion. Should I still keep in touch with her and possibly meet with her when I am in Bangkok or should I invite her to stop by?

If I said no, would it really matter? I don't think so.

Is there any possible danger in staying in touch with or meeting with her once again? What I do know for a fact is that she never asked me for any money except from that first time, plus I told her that I would never give her any money.

Like this matters?

She did indeed live in Sweden as I have seen her pictures and she knows basic Swedish. We do share the same humor. She has a very caring way of being towards me, and she is sharing Thai culture with me and she is teaching me Thai. She always emphasizes that I should learn and continue learning Thai. I like to learn about local stuff and I am an anti-tourist person. Moreover have I always looked down on these girls from bars and agree on many things you have been preaching in your videos.

I have joked with her that she should marry a European to get a foreign passport and work abroad and she has told me that she would not get married again, but she would not mind going abroad since she likes traveling. Overall, I have had a very loose approach and never indicated any interest in something serious or something like a relationship.

What do you think she is looking for? Money? Advice? Friendship? A relationship? Should I remain in contact with her? Can I see this as an exchange of Thai ways and local culture against supporting her emotionally or in Thai culture would a girl with her background be totally untrustworthy? I figured a guy like you would have some experience from Thailand and the stories you have heard please if you have the time fill me in.

Do you think one of those warnings will pop up if I continue to stay in touch with her? If you read this, I would greatly appreciate your input. If you have any questions, feel free, I am trying to understand all of this myself before I go ahead and freeze her out.

Could she possibly be a good person?

Best regards
Peter

***

Scott

Dude, this is a really long message but...wouldn't you rather be with a chick with a helluva lot less baggage? Like it or not, she is a bar girl with tons of baggage. After only seven days, you really do not know her. It sounds to me she's got you sprung (you are into her—too much so).

Is there any danger of meeting with her once? How do I know? But from what it sounds like she could whisper a few sweet nothings to you in bed, tell you what you want to hear, and you'll end up wanting more of her. You want to know if someone with her background is trustworthy. Decent women are sometimes untrustworthy, so what do you think? You are asking questions and you already know the answers. Man up and understand that like it or not, being with her is probably a losing proposition.

Scott

***

Peter

Thanks, I appreciate your taking the time to read it. It was a bit too long, I just wanted to have an opinion to confirm what I knew from the beginning, I guess. I must come across like an idiot, ha ha, ha. Better to cut it short. Anyway, you're doing good videos and stuff, keep it going.

Thanks,
Peter

***

Final Thoughts

The signs are as clear as day, but he is so deeply in love or lust he can't bear to see what is right in front of him. He even goes so far to ask me if I think a warning will pop-up if he continues to stay in touch with her.

Wake up pal, the writing is on the wall. She has a history of moving around and unsuccessful relationships, including at least one with a foreigner where she actually

227

moved to his country to be with him. Working as a masseuse in Korea and Malaysia, she's probably been ridden more than Secretariat and Seattle Slew combined.

He's talking about how caring she is towards him. Uggghhhh! Honestly, she's probably desperate to latch on to any halfway man who will have her. This seems to be her M.O!

I could be wrong, but if she's not in a relationship with him, she'll find some other sucker. More than likely, it's his turn, nothing more. She's worked in a massage parlor. At this point one could deduce she's just poor and thought this was a good way of making a living.

There are young women working in massage parlors that will refuse money for sex. Who knows, maybe she is a wonderful woman. However, worked in Korea and Malaysia and I doubt she traveled to these countries legally, simply to work in a traditional massage parlor. This definitely would have been enough to turn me off to any sort of relationship.

"For a period of time she had a Swedish boyfriend and tried living in Sweden."

Looking at this situation from the outside, with no emotional attachment, an intelligent man can see a pattern emerging.

"Could she possibly be a good person?"

This single question illustrates his naiveté and if I feel anything for this guy, it is sadness. Just as an office girl can be a horrible person, a bar girl or masseuse can be a good person; however, she is a person who for whatever reason decided to sell her body for a living. If this is acceptable, continue the relationship and see what happens. Men fail to realize what this entails and before they know it, they're in over their heads.

Only give what you are willing to lose because in my opinion, Peter's woman is no different from any other woman using her body to do the *George Jefferson.

*Doing the George Jefferson refers to the television show The Jeffersons. The intro music for the show, Movin' On Up, makes reference to George Jefferson movin' on up the social ladder from Queens, New York to the Upper East Side of Manhattan, also in New York.

Richard - What Is a Good Wife?

Richard

Hi Scott,

Sorry I haven't posted or written in a while. It was very nice to have your live stream on YouTube. I didn't know that was possible, but it is very neat to communicate with you in real time. Please keep going with that because it is definitely cool.

I'm still having heart problems and going to a cardiologist. My lung, my dick, etc., since I found out I have heart disease it's never ending. I take more than 20 pills a day and it's a task trying to keep up with all my appointments with various doctors. At the age of 56, it is crazy. I never expected these problems at my age. Nitro pills, blood pressure pill, and pills like Plavix to keep the new heart stents clear. Jesus, what is next?

I'm a bit jealous of you, because even after a hip replacement, which I also had done, you are still walking and filming. With my heart condition and low testosterone I am basically a limp dick, lol, with no juice.

Here's a question for you about Thai wives that has me puzzled. What do Thai wives think they need to do to be a good wife? To cook for you? To clean house? To take care of you and to have sex with you? What is a good American husband supposed to be like?

This is another one of those questions that is like asking, "How long is a piece of string?" or "How long

will it take me to become a great guitar player?" Is a wife expected to cook after she's worked a twelve hour day at the office? What about if she's a lousy cook? It's certainly nice to have a wife who cooks and cleans for you, but the role of women domestically, even Thai women, has changed over the years. Sex should be a part of every successful relationship. If the woman is staying home all day talking care of the children, then it would seem logical she does the cooking and cleaning for her man.

Scott to be honest, since my health condition I haven't been able to take care of the house and clean like I normally do because of my heart. I just don't have the energy I used to have. Yet, my wife has stopped cooking for me, and she hasn't started cleaning, inside or outside. She really never did anyway. She stopped sleeping with me, but she's done so because of my sleeping patterns. I really don't blame her, but you would think I would get some help from her. I really think she has given up on me. I don't want to be alone though with my health issues so this may be something to put up with, but I always thought a marriage was a partnership. Maybe with Thais it isn't or maybe I'm delusional.

If you have time I'd appreciate to hear from you.

Thanks.

***

Scott

I don't know your wife and I don't know her background. If she's from Isaan and was raised in a poor, dirty environment, her idea of what is acceptable and your idea might be different. You say you have talked to her about helping out more. Is there anything she asks you to do? You can't force her to do things she doesn't want to do. If you try this approach, she will end up hating you, or sick of you and resentful. I would sit her down, when she's relaxed, not right when she comes home from work, and ask her if she loves you. Assuming she says yes, ask her if she thinks she should help you around the house. If she tells you she already helps you, then you know you might have to adjust your thinking. Maybe you expect too much and maybe what she thinks she's doing is not enough to make you happy. Of course, make sure to tell her that with your heart condition it is getting much harder for you.

You can tell her that you love her, you are happy to be married with her, but you can also tell her that you would like her to help you out more—doing whatever.

You're telling me everything when the truth is you should be telling her you want to sleep with her, you want her to clean the house and do the dishes more, etc. Of course, stress the seriousness of your heart problem. If this doesn't work and you don't see a small change towards the direction you would like, then you know she is either unable to unwilling to do what you're asking. The trick is to figure out if she's unwilling or unable. If she is unwilling, then you have a problem.

From what you have told me, my guess is that she is working and tired, then sleeps in and wants a little time for herself. That takes up the majority of her time for four days a week. On her three days off, she probably wants to sleep in, do her laundry (unless you are doing it for her), or whatever. Give her time to herself, perhaps one day a week is enough. The other two days, she should spend with you and help do chores. She can hang out with her girlfriends on her one day to herself.

Let me make it clear, you need to communicate this to her, calmly, firmly and make sure she understands this is important to you. You might want to tell her you understand she needs her own time and that she is probably tired. If she doesn't respond, then when she needs something done, act exactly how she acts. Mirror her actions. That means putting yourself first and ignoring her requests. This is either going bring her to her senses and help her understand what you need, make her mad, or drive her away from you. Prepare yourself for any surprising answers or reactions.

Regards,
Scott

***

Scott,

Wow! You have great wisdom and experience and I want to thank you for that. No, I don't do her laundry and she doesn't do mine. Occasionally she does mine but I have so few clothes to do that I do my own. My wife never asks me to do anything, but I started picking up the place and just started doing the dishes on a regular basis. I use to let them sit, but I figured dishes would get done more by example and I was right. I don't mind doing the dishes even though she's the one who cooks six times a day and dirties the majority of the dishes. I decided by example was best and it proved to be helpful once she relied I wasn't trying to use her as a dishwashing slave, lol.

In the first letter, he said his wife has stopped cooking for him. Now he is saying she dirties the dishes

cooking six times a day!

My wife comes from a middle class people I believe. Their house was not bad; they made and sold clothes, had industrial sewing machines and also owned land with rubber trees. I really don't know how to judge her or her family. My wife is very religious though and she goes to the temple, meditates, and listens to the monks on the internet. She prays and meditates a lot, every day, in fact. I don't know if that helps you.

Your comments are very good and I thank you for them. Thanks Scott, you're a stand up guy.

Richard

***

Scott

Hey Richard,

I have asked you a couple of times what your wife does for a living and if she is at home most of the time. The more I think about it, the more important these things are. I personally don't care what she does and I'm definitely not judging your situation. But…if she's working a full time job, then she could be overwhelmed with things to do or think about. If she isn't working, there is no reason why she shouldn't be helping out, making life a little easier.

As I said in the last email though, you need to find a way to communicate this with her. Thai women are not always easy to communicate with and they have their own way of doing so. But you should try; it might help make the quality of your life a little better. I have had this discussion with my wife—long discussions. Thai women will not baby you, or give you sweet little kisses to make you feel better. They will and should make sure you are taken care and your needs are met. You are responsible for communicating those needs to her what you want and at times, it may necessitate being pushy. If she is getting from you at least some of what she wants, then it is only fair that you get some of what I want from her. A relationship is give and take and should be an equal exchange, or at least the majority of the time.

Anyhow, take care of yourself and if you feel like replying, do so. If not, get your rest, enjoy life and don't think too much.

Good luck,
Scott

***

Hey Scott,

Sorry it took so long to write. My wife works at a national massage company. She went to school, got her license and she now works from early afternoon until ten at night, four days in a row. The rest of the time she doesn't do much but watch television and go to lunch or hiking with her girlfriends. She also plays pickle ball once in a while. We have two houses and I don't get any help taking care of them. I would expect her to help me outside or cleaning or sweeping up once in a while, but nothing I have tried seems to work. I have asked for help, but I get no help. At this point we are like roommates. I try to invite her to do things with me, but I get turned down. But most of the time I haven't felt good, so I'm taking some responsibility for just not wanting to do anything. She used to cook for me all the time and now that is a rarity but then again, there were times I didn't like what she was cooking. She does know what I like though.

I hope this gives you a better picture.

Thanks,
Richard

Final Thoughts

Richard has contacted me in the past. In one of his emails, he complained about his wife being too religious. Because of her newfound dedication to Buddhism, their sex life had ceased, and as a man who loved his wife, he was unsure of what to say or do and how to approach the situation. I told him I thought he should put together a romantic evening and communicate his desire to reignite their sex life. A sexless marriage will only work if both partners are willing to do without.

It is difficult for me to tell him what to do and give him solutions, because I am only getting his side of the story. Maybe she is giving him all she has time to give. Perhaps she is giving more than he thinks. Maybe he is upset because of his medical issues and is lashing out at her. They have a daughter, so it is also quite possible she is worried about his physical condition and how she will raise their child should he pass away. Only they know the answers, but it would not surprise me if she is exhausted when she comes home and feels he is constantly pushing her to do more.

In the grand scheme of life, who does the dishes and the cooking and the cleaning are unimportant. Sometimes you have to focus on what is most important to the family, and while his frustrations are understandable, concentrating on spending quality time together as a family is most important.

Steve - Is Toilet Paper Better than Water?

Steve

Hey Scott,

I recently returned home from traveling around Cambodia with my Cambodian girlfriend.

One thing I noticed while we were staying in hotels is that the only time the level toilet paper went down is after I went to take a dump.

One time I walked past the bathroom while my girlfriend was in there, I heard the sound of a few turds dropping into the bowl, followed by a squirt of a high-pressure hose. This was then followed by a flush of the toilet.

This is truly one instance where I questioned my purpose on the planet. Surely my talents could be better used than to answer questions like this.

Next to the toilet, I would notice a very small amount of soiled paper in the trash bin. Obviously, I assume that my girlfriend does not clean her behind the same way most of us do in the west. I also don't think that what she is doing is a very hygienic practice.

I tried squirting the hose up my rear on one occasion for what seemed like a long time under high pressure and then used some paper to dry myself. I noticed that there was a lot of shit still left on the paper. I had to wipe

237

many more times from both rear to front direction and front to rear direction to remove all the crud from my rear end. I am curious to know if my girlfriend's bathroom habits are common amongst people living in Thailand as well.

Maybe he should have asked her, not me. I guess I should feel honored he wrote me with this problem, however I have to wonder about a man who is unable to figure out if his girlfriend has trouble cleaning her backside.

Honestly, I find it quite disgusting to think that my girlfriend is walking around every day blissfully unaware that she has shitty asshole!

I bet this makes him want to run out and have sex with her. Of course, cuddling is obligatory.

Oh yeah, over there people don't even call it toilet paper, they call it "tissue paper," LOL.

Thanks in advance,
Steve

***

Scott

Dude, not sure if you're messin' with me, but...she's your girlfriend! Don't you ever go down on her? If so and she didn't clean well, you ought to know it. There is nothing like the smell of shit to foul the pleasant aroma of a vagina primed for the taking. If she smells foul, determine where the nastiness is coming from and act accordingly. You are the one doing your thing with her, so a closer inspection and sniff test are certainly warranted.

Anyhow, I think the problem is probably your inexperience with the bum gun. I hate toilet paper now and never want to go back to using it. Those who know what they are doing rarely use the toilet paper other than to pat dry any excess water, but this is optional. If by chance you need to use your hand, just remember the left hand is for wiping, the right for eating and shaking.

Thanks for the video fodder,

Scott

All assholes are a little on the shitty side.
***

Steve

No mate, not messin' with you, and no, I don't go down on her. Haven't done that since '98 when I tried it on a black chick. The taste was so bad it made me puke and I had a sore throat for nearly three weeks! I actually think going down on a woman is quite a disgusting animal act to be honest, so avoid it now.

I thought I had used the bum gun for quite a long time so was very surprised that there was still some shit on the paper when I went to dry myself off. Took quite a few wipes before the paper wiped clean.

Funny that the folks in Cambodia think that those who use toilet paper are the dirty ones!

I challenge you to try folding the toilet paper over several times so that it won't tear and give your rear end several good hard wipes from both directions (rear to front and front to rear - this is important) after you have used the hose. I bet you that there will still be some shit left on the paper. You will need to wipe several more times until the paper wipes clean.

BTW, what does *puat kee puat tong sia* mean?

Thanks!

Steve

***

Scott

All vagina is different. Some is worth getting to know, some is better left untouched.

I'm not sure why you can't seem to clean your ass with a strong water stream. I never use toilet paper or tissue paper and believe me when I tell you, there are no remnants left on my ass nor do I have skid marks. If you have an exceptionally hairy ass, you might need to use your left hand to wipe. That's what soap and water is for.

I definitely understand the Cambodian (and Thai) mentality because I am completely sold on the bum gun. I hate toilet paper. You are dragging paper along your ass; this is the same as using a paper towel to wipe car grease off your hands. There are better ways to clean your hands and your ass crack and if you think about it, those wiping with toilet paper never quite get all the shit off until they take a shower. Use the spray gun properly and you'll be squeaky clean. To each is own, but when I'm in the West and no spray is available, I've gone so far as to wipe with the toilet paper, then hop into the shower to make absolutely certain I am squeaky clean. Toilet paper just scrapes off the top layer.

Puat kee – I need to shit so much it hurts.
Puat tong sia – I have diarrhea.

Scott

***

Steve

Right you are that all pussy is not the same. I developed a bit of an aversion to going down on women after my experience with the black chick! To be honest, I have been with three black chicks and all of them had strong, unpleasant body odor. Maybe it's just been my bad luck or maybe black women in general are just funky? Just a few months ago I was in the elevator and a black woman stepped in. She looked smoking hot but her body odor nearly floored me! I'm not talking about your typical BO smell that comes out the armpits; this was something different and more deadly!

I will try using the high-pressure hose next time I am in Southeast Asia and will report back.

Right now, I am in Australia and I gotta say some of the women here are smoking hot, but generally dumb as dog shit! Actually Aussies in general, although friendly, are mostly dumb as dog shit. Have you noticed the same?

Cheers mate!
Steve

Final Thoughts

This has to be one of the funniest, most disgusting letters I have ever received. I cannot imagine wondering if a woman I am involved with is walking around every day blissfully unaware that she has shitty asshole. If she is, she's had a really bad day or she doesn't care enough about herself and for me, that's a deal breaker and the relationship is over.

What I find even more amusing is that this guy is unable to figure out if his girlfriend is walking around with a shitty asshole and yet he has the gall to state, "Aussies are generally as dumb as dog shit." Like Steve is a shining example of a human being with vastly superior intelligence.

That said, I couldn't resist answering his emails. Maybe that says a lot for my own intelligence.

Teemu - My Goal Is To Be a Farmer

Teemu

Greetings Scott,

I have watched many of your videos on YouTube on the topic of living in Thailand. First of all, I would like to give big thanks for your comprehensive, concise and overall no-bullshit lessons on many of the issues surrounding the subject. It is greatly appreciated.

I am currently exploring the possibility of moving to Southeast Asia and am mapping out the obstacles. My goal would be to become a subsistence farmer so I have a source of income for additional security and to fund all the other things that I can't grow myself.

I am 31 years old and I have a girlfriend, so a Thai wife won't solve my problems. I have property worth 130,000 Euro that I would be selling to use the money to build a new life. I've never been to any part of Asia, but I am probably going to travel there soon to do some volunteering and get a little experience.

I've taken a superficial look at nearly all Southeast Asian countries (except for the island states), and Thailand would by far seem to be the best option. However, Thailand is giving me a headache with all its strict regulations and limitations imposed on foreigners.

First, and most obviously an obstacle, is the fact that agriculture is a prohibited activity to foreigners. Do you know if this applies to hand-to-mouth type of farming (self-sufficiency), or is it meant to protect the industry? Do you reckon self-sufficiency would be viewed as a threat to Thailand's economy? As a foreigner, I would essentially not input any money into the system due to a sort of food security independence, which essentially is exactly what I would strive for. In other words, maybe they prefer foreigners to buy the food from Thais. This is a potential deal breaker.

Another known obstacle is the land ownership laws. I don't conceptually resent having to just lease the land instead of owning it, and in terms of 30 year contracts extendable to 60 or 90 years, I don't see a problem. Assuming I am blessed with enough far-sighted consultation to avoid buying land that the government decides to build a road through or something.

Third, there is the permanent residency. Living with visa runs would quickly get ridiculous and annoying, so I would need to get permanent residency to actually live in Thailand permanently. The problem with this is that I don't have work experience nor education, so getting employed is difficult.

Do you know if volunteering counts as work, or do you have to get a paycheck to convince the officials that you can take care of yourself? This is kind of redundant were I to grow my own food. I could certainly consider getting a degree of some sorts, but at this point whatever new projects I start I would rather choose ones that help me achieve my goals. I have been thinking about starting a business too, but from what I've gathered the chances of reaching that 80,000 baht monthly income required for permanent residency are pretty slim.

Can you get a work permit visa for your own

company and are there specific requirements regarding employment of Thai nationals, revenue, paychecks, taxes and so on, to warrant getting PR in the end? Would the immigration bureau consider volunteer work a contribution to society and could it aid in getting PR?

Teemu is attempting to run before he can crawl.

Ideally I'd want a relatively simple life in the countryside, but close enough (40 miles or so) to a city. I would rather not be around tourists as I am looking to live a rather ascetic life. I am not a bar-goer or a party person. I am just looking for a good life where I am close to nature. I respect certain aspects of the Asian cultural fabric, hence my being drawn to it. I'm more of a perceptive than judgmental type, and I believe I could find my own space in this environment.

If you had the stamina to read all of my email and could give me any thoughts, reflections, advice, recommendations, I would very much appreciate it. If you think my plans would be easier to realize in another country, I'd like to hear all about it. The only no-no currently is living in the West.

Sorry about the verbosity, I know you have better things to do.

Thanks, regardless!

Teemu

***

Scott

Hello Teem,

You're not asking for much, are you?

Regards,

Scott

245

***

Hey Scott,

I certainly am.

It was a bit preposterous of me to think you'd give a detailed reply out of goodwill, it was just the impression I got from your videos.

I wasn't sure if you could offer advice on my kind of scenario, and if I were to purchase consultation time, I would want bang for my buck of course. I'd consider paying for consultation, but as it is I can't afford the rates.

What always gets me is when guys with such grandiose plans can't afford to pay $60 for an hour-long consultation. If you can't pay $60, how on earth are you going to make it to Thailand? I get message after message from guys like this and yet, very, very few ever pull the trigger.

If my situation changes and I can pay, I'll contact you.

All the best,
Teemu

***

Scott

Teemu,

I will tell you this…You cannot list your occupation as farmer and expect to be granted a work permit. Plant whatever you want to plant, eat it, give some to neighbors, but do not sell any of what you have grown. Anything a Thai can do, you can't, at least legally. Farming is obviously something Thais can do so you don't have a shot in hell at being a farmer and living off what you earn.

Volunteering is considered work. Immigration considers volunteering to be work, so technically you will be expected to have a work permit. Some people get away without one but...if you're considering living here long-term, getting a work permit is the way to go.

You cannot personally and legally lease the land. This is again, illegal. Cannot, as they say here in Thailand. Many people have set up Thai-owned companies that lease land, but even if you were able to do so, the lease would only be 30 years. The Thai government is cracking down on those flaunting the law, so beware of this. I wouldn't want to lose my land because of technicalities. You are a foreigner, you can't own land, simple as that.

The best you're going to do for a visa is an Education visa (ED) or perhaps a business visa if you can show you are looking into starting a business here. You might be able to do this but it's easier with a sponsor. If you apply for an ED visa, this does not count towards permanent residency. In order to apply for permanent residency, you need to have three one-year visas in a row.

If you start a company, you need four Thais for every foreigner who works for the company. Anytime you are working (or volunteering) you need a work permit. You need to pay taxes on all of the Thais working in your company. Immigration couldn't care less if you volunteer. It's not going to help you get a PR one bit.

There is a saying here, "They want our money but they don't want us." It is very true. Outwardly, Thais are polite and friendly. Once you live here a while you realize they are polite and friendly if you keep your relationship superficial and nothing threatens them. This is to be expected and most nationalities carry the same fear.

When it comes to the government being friendly, forget it, they'd be happiest if foreigners dropped off their money and left the country. Thais as a whole are not particularly fond of any nationality, especially those who threaten their livelihood or border their own country. If you're not Thai, you're an outsider, period. They'll tell you "Oh, now you are Thai," but this is nonsense. Thais are every bit as nationalistic as any other nationality. Can you blame them? Anyway, you either get used to it or learn how to ignore it or you leave.

This is a start. If you want more help, let me know when you are ready.

Good luck,
Scott

***

Teemu

Hey Scott,

Thanks for all the info. Leaves me with a lot to think about. I'll be doing more research and if I still see a window of opportunity and need further consultation, I'll be sure to get in touch. You seem to know your thing.

Again, big thanks.

Best wishes,
Teemu

Final Thoughts
One step at a time. K.I.S.S—keep it simple stupid.

Thailand attracts more than its fair share of dreamers, loners, wanderers and those looking to reinvent themselves. So it is completely understandable that Teemu wishes to live somewhere other than a Western country. However, desire alone is not enough. In order to fulfill his desire, he needs a plan that includes how to support himself. Throw out the plan to become a subsistence farmer.

Despite never having traveled to Asia and his rather simplistic dream of moving to Thailand to become a farmer, his contacting me probably saved him from huge disappointment, at least temporarily.

Immigrating to a foreign country is a huge step in a person's life and whether or not he follows through remains to be seen.

In my time living in Thailand I have learned much along the way, but probably the most basic tenet of moving to a foreign country is spending time inside the country prior to making the move. Then you get to know what is in store for you; if you're gonna play the game, learn the rules.

Update

Hello Scott,

In the nearly three years since we last spoke, my life situation has changed, introducing additional problems to consider. The most profound change in my life since we last talked is that there are now three of us!

I am still drawn to Southeast Asia and do want to travel there one day. We would stay for a few months though, not just a few weeks. This should still be realistic.

In the region, I'm most drawn to Laos. Thailand is definitely an option. Cambodia seems nice too, but I would probably feel too insecure there. Admittedly, it has been over a year since I've tried getting sense of the reality over there. Whichever the country we decide to try, what I'm currently most concerned about is our healthcare in case something unexpected happens. I've discussed it with my wife, so the idea is on the table (hopefully it won't stick to it).

Thanks again for the information you share.

Best wishes,
Teemu

Tommy - But She Works in a Dental Clinic

Tommy

Hi Scott,

My name is Tommy and I come from Sweden. I have traveled to Thailand for two months every winter for the past twelve years. I have only met bar girls, but the last two trips I have been with a girl who has a normal job. She works at a dental clinic in Pattaya. I thought this is a Thai girl that loves me for who I am and not for my money. During the first two years I traveled to Thailand and got to know her, she never asked me for money. I went home in March after a three month stay and everything felt so good. Then afterwards we talked every day on the phone for nearly two years. It was then I decided to send money to her.

Why? She has a job and earns what most Thais consider to be a decent wage for a single woman. Talking on the phone is different from physically spending time with a person. She has a job and unless they were engaged to be married—which means he should be able to trust her—there was no reason to start sending her money.

I remember when I said I would start sending money to her , she was crying so much and said she loved me more than her life.

The long wait finally paid off. Stop sending her money and see how fast she changes her tune.

In our talks, she told me about a Thai guy who had beaten her and now she hates Thai guys and will never be with one.

Okay, I feel for her, however…if an American man beats an American woman, will the woman swear off American men and only date foreigners? I doubt it.

Every day she went to Big C in Pattaya to eat food on her lunch break. I asked her why she would travel fifteen minutes by motorbike taxi every day from her job just to eat and her answer was that the food is good there.

Then I start to think!

It's about time. The one constant with most of the men who write me is they fail to see, or flat out disregard blatant warning signs.

There are usually restaurants or food stalls on the premises or within walking distance and most working Thai women opt to take their lunch close to their office. Her story might be understandable if there were no places to eat near her office. If every so often she needed a few items from Big C or wanted to meet a friend for lunch, this also is understandable. Spending half of her allotted time traveling back and forth to Big C because the food is good, is highly unlikely.

She admitted many foreign men go to Big C and often they came up to talk with her. Her story was that she would always tell them she has a boyfriend. We talked on Skype and Line every day, but suddenly she started using new apps that she wanted me to use. When I asked her who told her about these new apps, she said her friends recommended them to her.

Can you see where this is headed?

Then in August my friend's girlfriend saw her with a young *farang* at Big C. She saw my friend's girlfriend and told her that the man only was a friend she had just met and she was helping him with something.

Isn't she just the sweetest thing? I bet she wanted to make sure his pipes were thoroughly cleaned. She's looking for the bigger, better deal.

I called her and asked if she wanted to tell me something. She did not know that my friend's girl had already told me she saw her with a foreigner at Big C.

Then when I told her what I knew, she said, "Yes, yes, I was helping this man and then I went home."

This was in August and this is the month I stopped talking with her.

Then she sent me an e-mail and told me everything.

She met five different men after I went back home, but didn't have sex with them. She said they only met as friends.

Gullible sap.

The last man she met was Belgian and he is coming back to see her in January. She told me she only met him once to help him with a problem he had with the Thai police.

She sure is a helpful gal. Thai women are nice, but she's exceptional!

"Fucking bullshit," I said.

"Why would this man you helped and only saw once book a new ticket to come see you again?"

Then she copied a conversation she had with this man where she told him she loved me.

253

He told her she is stupid.

Then I asked her, "Hey if you only met this man once, how come he writes you all the time and spent all this money on a ticket to come see you?"

The answers are all there, he simply wants to believe that maybe, just maybe, he's wrong and she's as good as he wants her to be. Maybe she's different.

My question to you Scott is what type of girl is this? She has a good job with a good salary; she makes 15,000 baht every month. She said she hates Thai men and will never touch or fuck one. She has a silver ring on her finger with some Thai letters. I think she might have a Thai boyfriend, but when I come to Thailand, her phone never rings and she never receives any messages. Maybe she has another telephone for other *farang* or she calls them when she works?

Scott, I am not stupid, for sure I understand in my head that she has many other men and makes them send money to her, but I hate myself for trusting this girl. I don't think she's a bar girl and the last time I spoke with her she swore she didn't do anything with these men. I almost believe her.

But he's not stupid. He's different and it's all the other guys who are clueless. He's a Chowderhead and he desperately wants to believe her.

She said she only met this man from Belgium once and I believed her until I saw the conversation between them.

I changed my Swedish phone number and blocked her everywhere so she can't contact me, but I still think in my head Scott, maybe she speaks the truth. How fucking stupid am I?

So which is it, he's stupid or he's not stupid? Personally, I think he is an idiot and this relationship has way, way too much drama.

In January, I'll go to Thailand again, but I promised myself I would not contact this girl. It is better for me to go to a real bar girl then a fake bargirl, hahaha.

Thanks for reading this and I hope you will answer.

Take care,
Tommy

***

Hi Tommy,

Thanks for writing.

This is one reason I say not to hook up with any women in Pattaya. The city is a whore town and even the so-called good girls or girls with mainstream jobs learn quickly foreigners give them many options. If they're decent looking they can take their pick from men and make easy money.

From what you have told me, she has demonstrated the type of woman she is. I wouldn't give her a second chance.

Her version of love is much different from yours and it's never going to change. She met five men behind your back and while she claims she did not have sex with them, you will always wonder if she was telling the truth. Cut her loose and forget her. Sometimes it takes going through several women before you met a truly good one.

All the best,
Scott

***

Tommy

Thank you so much Scott,

I have learned my lesson now. Rule number four, never fall in love in Pattaya. Yes, of course, she learned from other girls why she does not need to work hard every day. Better to get some *farang* to give her money.

I don't know where to look for a good Thai lady and now I don't believe there are any out there for me. Now what do I do? Maybe I should give her a second chance.

Take care and I hope to meet you in Bangkok someday. I'll buy you some beer and thank you for your advice.

All the best
Tommy

***

Final Thoughts

Hopefully, he learned his lesson. Tommy is another example of a man blinded by the power of exotic love and sex. The writing was on the wall, the red flags are everywhere, and yet he is willing to allow this woman into his life. She's an untrustworthy pain in the ass, nothing more.

So what would I have done?

If I felt like it, I would have screwed her, gave her a few bucks, and never believed a word she said. Once back in Sweden, where Tommy hails from, I would not send her any money.

If Tommy did this, at the very least she might respect him. Not that this really matters.

No sweet talking, no I love you honey, no long talks on Skype; she deserved nothing more than a phone call or message to set up a roll in the sack. Once tired of her body, say goodbye and never speak with her or see her again. To some it might sound coldhearted, but the truth is, he owes her absolutely nothing.

Tony - I Lost My Best Friend to a Thai Prostitute

Tony

Hi Scott.

I want to apologize in advance because this is letter is going to be a pretty long letter. Allow me to provide a little background. While in the Navy, I became good friends with this guy who was going through a bad divorce. He married a Japanese woman, she ended up divorcing him and pretty much left him to start over.

Maybe three weeks after his divorce, he went to the Philippines, found a Go-Go girl in a bar there and started a relationship with her. Two weeks after meeting her, he managed to get her pregnant. Lucky for him she had a miscarriage. He started sending her money monthly and decided that he wanted to marry her.

Already this guy sounds screwed up.

All the people in command tried to have an intervention to persuade him not to do it. Eventually they decided to grant his request to marry her, but as an end result, they pulled his security clearance. He had been under investigation for something unrelated, but they had no findings and decided they were going to give his clearance back. However, due to his weird choice, they decided maybe he shouldn't get his clearance back. This led to him getting kicked out of the Navy.

He took his Filipino back to rural Indiana in America and the relationship quickly deteriorated. When a girl is living the farm in the Philippines, she doesn't expect to end up on another farm. The relationship ended with her being spiteful, mostly due to boredom, then he asked her to contribute to paying their household expenses. After getting her green card, she took an extended trip to see her sister back in the Philippines and just decided to never come back.

During this time, I convinced him there was nothing left to salvage. She wasn't going to give him any closure. She moved on with her life and found a new relationship. I told him that it would be better to start divorce proceedings and move on or risk falling into depression. This is approximately four years after he got kicked out of the Navy. When he got out, he got a general discharge. Because of this, I persuaded him to try to get disability from the VA and then come to Thailand to use the GI Bill to go to Webster University Campus in Cha-am. He went for his VA appointments and found that he was deaf in one ear and needed to have surgery and that he would get 70% disability.

70% disability at E-5 with dependents, plus BAH from the GI Bill and rent for his house would net him around $3,000 a month. I told him that he was set up nicely. All he needed to do was come here and go to school. Five months before the term starts and before he would be arriving in Thailand, we spoke on the phone pretty much every day. The conversations were mostly of him asking me to tell him the mistakes I made here so that he would not make the same ones. I told him to be careful dealing with the woman, not spend too much time in the bars and to remember there were many normal women running around.

Anyway, I moved to Bangkok to take a job and now had two places to live, so I offered to let him rent my car and apartment in Hua Hin for 10,000 baht a month. The apartment was fully furnished and the car was in good condition. I advised him to keep his expenses low so he could enjoy traveling and not have too many obligations. Fast forward to his arrival, my girlfriend and I picked him up from the airport and he stayed at our condo in Bangkok. For the first week everything seemed pretty normal. It was unfortunate that I had quit my job around the time of his arrival, which meant that I would not be able to party hard with him. That upcoming weekend, I took him to Pattaya because he had never been there and on the first day we drank and hung out, not really spending much time in the go-go bars, mainly giving him the lay of the land. The next day we walked down Soi 6 where we were invited into a bar by two young Thai girls. We went in and spent an hour or so there. I didn't pay the girl much attention (been there, done that) instead playing music from YouTube at the bar while he conversed with his new companion.

At eight, he asked the girl if she wanted to go out and she said yes. She wanted to go to Insomnia, so we took both girls and got pissed drunk. In the morning, I woke up knocked on his door to get him up before checkout time. We met at a British pub around the corner for breakfast. After breakfast we settled our bill and when I went to look for a taxi, my friend said, "We can't go yet." I asked why and he said because we needed to wait for the girl. She would be going back to Bangkok with us. I thought it was weird but okay, no big deal, he was probably going to continue to smash it for a while before sending her back.

We get to Bangkok condo and start to drink. Then, much to my surprise, he tells me the girl is going to live with him in Hua Hin.

This guy is a Chowderhead. Absolutely no brains.

"That's good, I guess, but don't you think that's a little too fast?" I ask.

If he were my friend, I probably would have got in his face and asked him WTF he was doing! At the very least I would have called him an idiot and tried to shake him out of his mental fog. This guy doesn't need a bar girl, he needs a psychiatrist.

Anyway, I don't say anything else about it. The next day he and the bar girl start arguing, he is upset because she no longer wants to move to Hua Hin with him. In the course of their argument, I find out this is because he doesn't have enough money to send to her family every month. She tells him that she sends home a minimum of 50,000 baht every month and if he can't send this much, she can't be his girlfriend. I told him it is not going to work, he should just enjoy his time with her and then let her go when she wants to leave. He keeps pushing the issue until he upsets her and she leaves.

At this point it dawns on me that the reason for her coming and going is because we went to Pattaya on a Buddhist holiday and there was no work for her. She came with us to see what she could gain and now she's off to work again. The next day, my girlfriend returns from visiting her family and she tells him that we met on the dating app Skout. She recommends he try Skout, because more educated Thai women are on there.

Skout is definitely not what he needs and I question the friend and the friend's girlfriend's judgment. Seriously, with his track record, why put a decent woman through the anguish.

He seems to have a bad habit of sinking his fangs into any girl who gives him the opportunity!

The next day, he gets a cell phone, installs the app and start chatting. The following day he finds out that he caught gonorrhea from the bar girl he brought from Pattaya. I flip out, because when he was in America I asked him to bring me condoms (because Thai size is small) and he brings condoms for me but not himself. Instead he got a vasectomy. Anyway, we go to the pharmacy to meds and he says that he learned his lesson.

And he believes this why? I wouldn't believe anything the guy says!

The following day, he says he made a date with a girl from Skout. He goes out and then this becomes the remainder of his stay. He wakes up, eats and says, "Hey dude, I have a date, I'm out."

My girlfriend is upset because he's turned our condo into a hotel; some nights he will come home alone and other nights he will bring home a girl. I tell my girlfriend that he just got out of a nasty divorce and to cut him some slack, but then at 3AM one morning he brought home a Nigerian hooker and I had to tell him to chill out. The following night he gets a message from a Thai girl at 2AM and she asks him to come over. So he asks if I can wake my girlfriend up to help him get a taxi to go to her apartment. I tell him no, instead taking him to the main road where I flagged one down for him. I told him to be careful and sent him on his way. At 6AM he comes home and has brought this girl with him.

"Who is this?" I ask.

She's going to live with me in Hua Hin," he said.

I was mortified. For me that was the last straw. I told my girlfriend to pack some clothes for us, because we would be taking him to Hua Hin. When we were ready to leave, my friend asks me to take him to exchange money; we went to Sukhumvit because that was the only place that would take dirty dollar bills. The money exchangers on Ratchadapisek Road won't take your bills unless they're pristine. Anyway, he and I go to Asoke and change his bills. When we return to the condo, the girl is gone. I asked my girlfriend what happened to the girl and she told me the girl said she had some business to attend to and that she would meet him in Hua Hin. So we go to Hua Hin without her.

Anytime the drama starts ramping up as it did with this bonehead, it is time to re-evaluate the relationship.

We drop him at the apartment to get settled in and then the next day we take him out for seafood in Cha-am. When we arrive to Cha-am, he asks me if I have a Thai bank account. I ask him why does he need a Thai Bank account and he tells me that he and the girl have been messaging on the phone and he needs to send her 5,000 baht so she can take the bus to Hua Hin.

I tell him that a bus from BKK to Hua Hin costs 180 baht to send her only 1,000 but he insists and we finally settle on 3,000 baht. He gives me the money, I put it in my account and when I am in the process of sending it my girlfriend notices that the receiver is a Thai man. My friend says he doesn't care and sends it anyway. This pissed me off, because when he stayed at my condo in Bangkok he only paid for lunch and dinner once. When a booty call asks him for money to travel, he doesn't think twice about sending 5,000 baht! After the receiving the money, the girl says that she can't come today and she would come the next day. My girlfriend and I go back to Bangkok because she has to work, but we return on Friday. When we arrive in Bangkok, we go to our favorite Thai restaurant and see my friend drunk, screaming because this chick hasn't shown up yet and she is suddenly not answering his phone calls.

Drama after drama, stupidity after stupidity; neither of these guys, nor the girlfriend are very intelligent.

He tells me that she said she would go to the bar to drink with her friends and family and now is not answering. He called her so many times the killed the battery on his phone. My girlfriend and everyone at the restaurant—no exaggeration—try persuading him to forget about her. There are many other women in Hua Hin. He is drunk, but he decides to hop on a motorbike to go home to charge his phone so he can continue calling her. At this point I am embarrassed, this is my friend and I introduced him to everyone and now he is behaving like this.

As well he should be embarrassed!

The next morning the girl shows up and I try getting him to let her go, but he tells me he will have fun with her and then let her go. The following weekend I come to Hua Hin, not to hang out with him, but to go to the beach and relax with my girlfriend. One of my Thai friends who is helping my friend out because of his new guy status, pulls me to the side and tells me the girl is not a good girl. My friend and girl are both from Isaan and they have talked at length. She told him that she has a kid; she used to be a prostitute in Phuket. On many occasions has referred to my friend as a retard because he is deaf in one ear. My Thai friend wanted me to talk to my friend for him about this because his English skills weren't good enough to articulate it.

Later on that day, when I am alone with my friend, I talk to him about what was said.

"That's not what she told me," he said.

I told him about her calling him a retard he would not accept what I was saying. Eventually he and the girl get into an argument and she leaves. He goes back to his routine of meeting girls on Skout and in the bars. The following weekend I meet with my Thai friend who proceeds to tell me that he has invited my friend to dinner several times and each time my Navy buddy brought a bar girl.

And this is surprising why?

My Thai friend feels uncomfortable with a prostitute being around his wife and son. I tell my Thai friend that I have no control over what he does, but I will talk to him. I also told him that maybe it is best not to hang out with him. Again I talk to my buddy, not about what I was told, but I tell him not to alienate himself from people. I also try to tell him about how many guys come here and get so caught up in pussy and drinking they tend to push the good people away. He fails to see how his actions could push people away.

Around this time, I start a new job and stop going to Hua Hin as often. He and I talk on the phone and when we talk, it's always about a girl that he met. Everything that he said he wouldn't do when he got here, he is doing. My girlfriend decides that she will go home to visit her sick grandmother leaving me with a free weekend. I call my friend on Monday to let him know that I am free and we can hangout. I suggest we go to Pattaya, to the countryside, or anywhere.

"Man, I have a girl here," he said.

"That's why I'm letting you know in advance," I said, irritated.

"I really like her though and want to make it work."

I just lost it, because the day before yesterday he was talking the same way about a different girl. Two days later he has a girl that he wants to make it work with? WTF?

"I don't want to go to Pattaya, because no girl is that stupid. She'll know why I'm going there."

"Dude, why does everything have to be about whores and sex? Why don't we just hang out with me? We haven't seen each other for seven years!"

He then says that if it were me and my girlfriend he would give us space to fix out relationship.

This is too much for me to handle. One idiot thinks he's in love with every woman stupid enough to be with him and the other moron leads him straight into battle. The guy doesn't need to go to Pattaya, he needs a therapist! Seriously!

The one thing that I hate about foreigners in Thailand is when they date a whore and try to compare their abnormal relationship to a normal relationship.

Honestly, I'm not sure this guy's relationship with his own girlfriend is all that normal!

I told him that the beginning of my relationship was

not based on having sex and my girlfriend wasn't causing me or the people around me any grief.

He then took a cheap shot at me.

"You are a divorcee, how can you give advice?"

"I got divorced, but I learned from my mistakes, you're repeating a pattern." I told him that I got tired of feeling like the veteran foreigner that needs to show the new foreigners the ropes. It seems like people want to be around me because I know a lot about Thailand, but once they get what they need, they stop wanting to hang around you.

He said that if I feel like that, then nothing is wrong with the other people, something is wrong with me.

Stupid and stupider.

He then admitted that the girl that he was with was the same girl that had been calling him a retard. At that point I asked why he was so desperate and why was he trying to be with women who did not reciprocate his feelings. There were plenty of girls that he dated that seemed a lot more suitable. He dated many women that were more attractive, held good jobs and were independent, but he always chose to be with young prostitutes.

After this conversation he and I stopped talking. A week later I got a call from security at my Hua Hin apartment. They told me the police had been called to my apartment. I had my girlfriend call my Thai friend, who quickly found out my Navy buddy and his girl were fighting over her talking to another man on her cell phone. The girl asked security to call the police.

I sent him a message and got no response. Five minutes later, I see that my Line message was read, but that there was no answer. I told my friend that I needed to talk in order to make sure that everything was okay. After all, it is my apartment and I am responsible. He did not answer. When my girlfriend got home from work, she told me that my friend had called my Thai friend, yelled at him, and then called her and yelled at her. The guy told my girlfriend I was angry because he wouldn't go to Pattaya with me and that if she believes I only go to Pattaya just to drink and party, she's stupid. He also tells her he will be moving out of my apartment on the first. II told him we didn't need to talk, but that I will come to Hua Hin on the first to get the apartment and car keys. I just want to make sure that there are no misunderstandings because it's a long drive.

"Okay, just make sure you have a refund for the advanced rent that I paid you," he said.

I tried to call him to talk to him about it, letting him know that I am not kicking him out that and he is the one who said he was leaving, but he ignores my calls and messages.

All of this drama is just painful!

The next morning I drive to Hua Hin from Bangkok to confront him. When I get there, he opens the door and greets me.

"What do you want?" he said.

"Dude, what the fuck is your problem?" I said. "All of this drama over a bitch? Yelling at people over a bitch? Are you fucking serious?"

I told him the girl can't stay because of all of the issues she is causing. I open the door to tell her to pack her things and go and he grabs me. I start punching and kicking him and then I try to choke him out. During all of the commotion I notice that he is playing on her phone while I'm stomping him out. He yells "Baby, call the police!"

She ignores him. He then says, "Baby, go next door, go to the neighbor's apartment!"

She causally gets dressed, walks out and goes down the hall. When I let him up he goes chasing after her.

"Baby, where are you going?"

It was pathetic to watch. This chick clearly cared nothing for him, but he's chasing after her. I calmed down, talked to him and told him it is better he goes his way and I go mine. The next day he confirms he is moving out and that's it.

When he came to Thailand I thought I was getting a long lost friend back, there were so many things that we were supposed to do when he got here, but he got obsessed with pussy to the degree that a drug addict gets addicted to heroin. My going into the bedroom to ask the girl to leave was the equivalent to take a needle from the junkie.

I am writing this because I listen to a lot of letters that you read Scott and they are almost always from the viewpoint of the person with the addiction who needs to be loved. These people don't realize that in their desperate pursuit of love they lose the people that really do love and care for them. This month my friend lost a friend of 11 years (me) for a girl he has seen about 12 times. Eventually she'll go her own way and he'll be left trying to fill an empty space with meaningless relationship after meaningless relationship. Trying to force puzzle pieces to fit where they don't.

P.S. Thanks, if you took the chance to read this, it

269

means a lot.

Tony

***

Scott

The writing was on the wall when he hooked up with the Filipina whore. It sucks he caused problems for you at your place. This is uncalled for and friend or not, it was definitely grounds for booting him.

That said, had you not let him live there, you could have just told him you're his buddy and you care for him and think he is screwing up, but he's going to do what he's going to do. We can be friends and I will be there for you, but I don't want anything to do with your relationships.

Or you could take one of my lines.

"I don't get involved in matters of the heart."

You can lead a horse to water, but you can't make him drink. Maybe one day he'll come to his senses. From the looks of his relationship history though, I wouldn't count on it.

Scott

***

Tony

Thank you for the reply. It's sad, I've talked to people who found themselves in similar situations and sadly, it takes something drastic to wake them up; HIV, angry Thai boyfriends, or depression to name a few things. It seems life punching him in the face will be the only thing he responds to and by then it will be too late. Three days ago he phoned me and told me that the chick started acting crazy and when he tried to boot her, she informed him that she is not 18 years old but actually 16 years old. If he breaks up with her she will cry rape. He wanted my advice on how to handle the situation and I told him that he made his bed and that he had to lie in it. I also told him to please stop bothering me and my Thai friends with his dysfunctional relationships. I hate that I had to do this, but only contacting me when he has a relationship issues is bullshit.

Final Thoughts

Dating and relationships should be fun, but for some, like Thai working girls trying to make a buck, getting involved with a man is serious business. Men fail to understand the seriousness of their interactions with women who are hell bent on making a better life for themselves with their money. A relationship with a Thai prostitute can quickly destroy love, marriage, a family, and as demonstrated in the above case, a friendship. In some cases, it even can cost a man his life.

These two guys are clearly knuckleheads. Friends stand by their friends, but friends do not unnecessarily and foolishly burden their friends with nonsense. Life is too short. Better to have one or two quality friends than ten friends who are a huge pain in the ass. Mr. Navy guy isn't a friend, he's a festering boil on his buddy's ass. Fortunately, this boil has now been excised.

Update

Hi Scott,

I sent an email to you in August about a Navy buddy of mine that I convinced to moved to Thailand. I just wanted to give an update. I spoke to a mutual friend today in passing and found out that his gonorrhea was not treated and had gotten worst in the past few months. It has gotten to the point where the he had to stay in the hospital for a couple of days. The doctor told him that if it doesn't improve that they're going to have to amputate his penis. This leave me feeling bad because in the back of my mind I kept saying to myself that if he continues on the same course he is going to end up catching something that he can't get rid of or end up getting himself killed. I feel like I watched him get on a plane that I knew was going to crash. So, he's left by himself while the chick has moved on. She went back to working in the bar and now he is showing up to the bar where she works telling her that he wants to be reimbursed for everything that he has done for her. I see many friendships here end like mine over pussy. My friend is now left with an STD, no friend and no "girlfriend."

***

Scott

Your friend is an idiot. It's sad, but this sort of thing happens. If losing his pecker doesn't jar him into reality, nothing will.

Scott

ASK
ME
ANYTHING

Scott Mallon was born in 1962 in Coral Gables, Florida. In 1982, he moved to Southern California where he worked for 13 years as printing press operator and job estimator before deciding to sell everything to jump on a jet bound for Thailand.

His first book, *They Call Me Farang, Short Stories by An American in Bangkok*, reached number one on Amazon and quickly became a must-have for those interested in Thailand.

Prior to writing *They Call Me Farang,* Mallon worked as a boxing and travel photojournalist for over fifty publications, including HBO Sports, the Bangkok Post, The Ring, Boxing Digest, Boxing News, The Fist and the Phuket Gazette.

He lives full time in Bangkok with his Thai wife Beau, their sons Alex and Nicholas and dogs Lala and Odie.

Printed in Great Britain
by Amazon